WOULD YOU YOU RATHER?...

ultimate

SEX

edition

Over **700**
Ludicrously
Lustful Dilemmas
to Ponder

Justin Heimberg
& David Gomberg

Published by Seven Footer Press
247 West 30th St., 11th Fl.
New York, NY 10001
10 9 8 7 6 5 4 3 2
Printed in the United States of America

Design by Thomas Schirtz

ISBN 978-1-934734-99-5

www.sevenfooterpress.com

How to Use This Book

Sit around with a bunch of friends and read a question out loud. Discuss the advantages and drawbacks of each option before making a choice. Stretch, twist, and otherwise abuse your imagination to think of the multitude of ways the choice could affect you. The question is merely a springboard for your conversation.

Everybody must choose. As the Deity proclaims, YOU MUST CHOOSE! Once everyone has chosen, move on to the next question. It's that simple.

If you receive a question directed at females, and you are male (or vice-versa), you can do one of several things: a) move on to another question, b) answer the question anyway, or c) freak out.

On occasion, we have provided some "things to consider" when making your decisions, but do not restrict yourself to those subjects when debating. There are no limits with this book, so go ahead and get down and dirty. Say whatever is on your mind no matter how repugnant and nasty. There are few forums where one gets to express their deviant and warped side, so please let loose.

Introduction

Sex.

It's what drives everything. Blame Darwin. Natural selection resulted in sex becoming one of the most pleasurable activities known to man, right up there with popping bubble wrap. Any cave people who engaged in sexual intercourse, and shrugged an indifferent "eh" before returning to the joys of skinning mammoth were weeded out of the human race because they ignored the call of persistent mating. Humans need to procreate; so doing it better feel good. That makes sense.

It's harder however to understand how natural selection explains a foot fetish, or the need to dress up as a baseball umpire to get off. What sort of evolutionary stable strategies are these? How does depositing one's ejaculate on another's foot perpetuate one's genes? Oral sex? Anal sex? Nasal sex? None of these lead to gene-preservation. And so proponents of Intelligent Design might point to the current sexual climate as evidence against evolution. And yet, what exactly is intelligent about the endless array of perversions and sexual hang-ups peppered throughout hundreds of different cultures?

In fact, the mechanics of sex—two sensitive vulnerable dangling balls, the befuddling clitoris, hideaway g-spots, the fact that we pee out of the same hole we ejaculate from—this pretty much refutes the notion of Intelligent Design and instead invites images of a lazy Deity, waiting until the day before the assignment is due, rushing to get his civilization done, sacrificing the finer points; to wit, grotesque purposeless mounds of pubic hair. Sex isn't so simple, in the end. That Sex Ed teacher who reduces sex to its most basic operation is secretly thinking about being bound in twine, slapped with a flounder, and being called "Maestro."

Sex, like the meaning of life itself, is best left open and unanswered, to be explored rather than explained, to be made personal rather than universal. And so, we offer this book as a means of exploring your sexuality along with that of your friends—a chance to delve into the hypothetical and imaginative to better define where you stand sexually (or squat, or lay, or crouch). So worry not about revealing something a little seedy about yourself. You're not alone.

These are the circumstances: A Deity descends from on high and informs you that, for reasons beyond your understanding, your sex life is about to change. From this moment on, regarding matters of flesh and heart, you are to be bestowed with a terrible curse, an unusual perversion, an unlikely power, an embarrassing circumstance, or some other sexual oddity. The Deity is not without compassion, however. Ever a believer in human free will, he allows you to choose between two possible fates. **But choose you must.**

Would you rather...

never experience orgasm

OR

perpetually experience orgasm?

Things to consider: business meetings, funerals, public speaking

Would you rather...

come home to find your parents reading your diary

OR

reading *The Kama Sutra*?

YOU MUST CHOOSE!

Would you rather...

have sex with Victoria Beckham if she gained 60 pounds

OR

if she lost 20 pounds?

Would you rather...

passionately make out with a heavy drooler

OR

give oral sex to a heavy farter?

YOU MUST CHOOSE!

Would you rather have sex with...

Eva Mendes **OR** Kim Kardashian?

Friday Night Lights' Minka Kelly **OR** Jaime Pressly?

an unenthusiastic Laura Conrad **OR** a down-and-dirty Nancy Pelosi?

Natalie Portman **OR** Jennifer Lopez if they had each other's butts?

classy Christina Aguilera **OR** slutty Christina Aguilera?

YOU MUST CHOOSE!

Would you rather have sex with...

Johnny Depp **OR** Brad Pitt?

50 Cent **OR** Dr. Drew?

Matthew Fox **OR** Jake Gyllenhaal?

Jimmy Kimmel **OR** Mitt Romney?

a first cousin of your choice **OR** John Madden?

YOU MUST CHOOSE!

Would you rather live in a world where...

condoms were able to magically crawl out of the wrapper and put themselves on exactly at the right moment

OR

there was a male contraceptive pill that caused some bloating and moodiness?

YOU MUST CHOOSE!

Would you rather...

have genitalia that whistles like a tea pot when you get turned on

OR

genitalia that emits a loud buzz and flashes a *Family Feud* "X" when you're turned off?

YOU MUST CHOOSE!

Would you rather have sex with...

Angelina Jolie **OR** Megan Fox?

Halle Berry **OR** Heidi Klum?

Reese Witherspoon **OR** Elisabeth Hasselbeck?

George Clooney **OR** Kirstie Allie at her heaviest/sloppiest?

Would you rather...

receive a Twitter tweet every time your partner has sexual thoughts about another person

OR

not?

YOU MUST CHOOSE!

Would you rather...

be unable to refrain from spastically "freaking" anyone you see over 70 years old

OR

upon saying goodbye, be unable to refrain from patting people on the butt with a friendly tap and a wink?

Would you rather have sex with...

Jessica Simpson if she gained 100 pounds *OR* Helen Mirren?

Jessica Alba and get herpes *OR* Meredith Viera and get a new Xbox?

A limbless Adriana Lima *OR* Joy Behar?

YOU MUST CHOOSE!

Would you rather...

have clitoris-level sensitivity all over your body

OR

be capable of shooting pubic "quills" in self-defense like a porcupine?

Would you rather...

have your entire sexual history be re-enacted by the animatronic robots in a Disney World ride á la the Pirates of the Caribbean?

OR

have the characters in your sex life released by the Franklin Mint as collectable pieces of a commemorative chess set?

YOU MUST CHOOSE!

Would you rather...

have the sounds of your love-making uploaded every day on iTunes

OR

have a video of you in the throes of masturbation posted on YouTube?

Would you rather...

have upside-down genitals

OR

your genitals moved three inches to the left?

YOU MUST CHOOSE!

Would you rather...

have your wedding videographer be Joe Francis (creator of *Girls Gone Wild*)

OR

have your wedding ceremony officiated by Flavor Flav?

Would you rather...

have "innie" nipples

OR

inch-long, curly, "elf-shoe" nipples?

YOU MUST CHOOSE!

Would you rather have sex with...

Kate Hudson **OR** Anne Hathaway?

Hayden Panettiere **OR** Mila Kunis?

Christina Ricci **OR** Scarlett Johannson?

Would you rather...

see in ColecoVision graphic quality when having sex

OR

have to use clinical terms during dirty talk? (for example, "Penetrate that vagina!" ; "Lick that mons pubis!"; "Ram that glans against the epidermis of the uvula!")?

YOU MUST CHOOSE!

Would you rather have sex with...

The Rock **OR** Denzel Washington?

Bono **OR** Sting?

the Jonas Brothers **OR** the Baldwin Brothers?

Justin Timberlake **OR** Kanye West?

John Mayer **OR** Jack Johnson?

YOU MUST CHOOSE!

Would you rather have...

9 inch nipples **OR** a 9 inch clitoris?

a 24 month menstrual cycle **OR** a 24 hour menstrual cycle?

a 4 pound tongue **OR** a 4 pound testicle?

Would you rather...

find out your spouse has genital warts

OR

that they are having an affair? With your sibling? With your best friend? With Tito Santana?!

YOU MUST CHOOSE!

Would you rather...

have sex with a 10 **OR** two 5s? (5s are at the same time)

a 10 **OR** ten 1s?

a 10 with syphilis **OR** a 4 with nice high-thread count sheets?

a 10 and a -3 **OR** a 5?

Siamese twin 10s **OR** just one 10?

$10^2 \cdot (2 + \sqrt{125/9}\,)$ **OR** $2^{4(32 - .65)}$?

Things to consider: order of operations

YOU MUST CHOOSE!

Would you rather...

orgasm once every 20 years

20 Years – Justin Heimberg

If you orgasm ever 20 seconds, you simply cannot function in life. Imagine that Power Point presentation at work. Your wedding day. Your wedding night. Funerals. Parenting. And don't say you'd get used to it and be able to muffle your ecstasy. If that were the case, we'd all be used to it by now. After our first dozen or so, we'd orgasm with humdrum nods of approval without a varied breath, not cross-eyed facial pandemonium coupled with sounds we are otherwise incapable of. You never get used to an orgasm. That's why we need more. Almost constant orgasm would cast you out of society, and there you would stay, lying in a gutter somewhere in a pool of your own goods, the happiest bum in the world.

YOU MUST CHOOSE!

OR once every 20 seconds?

20 Seconds – David Gomberg

Buy me some specially lined pants, because there is no way you can go through life orgasming every 20 years. This goes beyond being a bit cranky. You'd go crazy. You'd murder. Steal. You'd write a horrible off-Broadway play. And in a sense, yes, the orgasms you actually have will be intense, perhaps producing enough ejaculate to power a small exurb; but when, where, and why will they come? That's real pressure to get that moment right. For men, if you are looking to reproduce, you'd need to can that sucker in a golden urn and protect it like a holy seminal shroud. Take the mess. It's worth it. No worse than a runny nose. It's just like having a cold of the crotch.

YOU MUST CHOOSE!

Would you rather...

have sex with Tom Brady and get herpes

OR

have sex with Tom Brokaw and get a sensible but stylish tote bag?

Would you rather...

have sex with Jenna Jameson and get crabs

OR

have sex with Katie Couric and get a nice pair of business-casual wrinkle-free slacks with solid craftsmanship?

YOU MUST CHOOSE!

Would you rather be forced to always have sex...

to the soundtrack of *High School Musical* **OR** festive Indian music?

in strobe light **OR** with NASCAR airing in the background?

in libraries **OR** in janitorial closets?

Would you rather...

be able to achieve orgasm at will

OR

be able to make anyone other than you achieve orgasm at your will?

Things to consider: public speakers, staff meetings, sporting events

YOU MUST CHOOSE!

Would you rather...

acquire all the knowledge of people you have sex with

OR

right before you climax, have the choice to store up orgasms to experience later, like the "downloading later" function on email?

Things to consider: rainy days, orgasm breaks at work, nerd-banging

Would you rather have all of your sexual dreams directed by...

Jerry Bruckheimer *OR* Judd Apatow?

the Wachowski brothers *OR* the Coen brothers?

David Lynch *OR* Pixar?

YOU MUST CHOOSE!

Would you rather...

orgasm every time your cell phone rings

OR

have your cell phone ring every time you are about to orgasm?

Would you rather...

always have sex standing up

OR

without ever facing one another?

Would you rather...

(men read as "date someone with...")

have no vagina

OR

have 17 vaginas all over your body?

YOU MUST CHOOSE!

Would you rather change your name to...

(women, read as "marry and take the name of")

Derrick Fingerblast

OR

Ronald Queefcloud?

Would you rather...

be able to blow visible kisses across a room

OR

be able to fart directionally with an accuracy of 40 feet?

YOU MUST CHOOSE!

Would you ever have sex...

in a dressing room stall at the mall?

in a car in a public parking lot?

in your parents' bed?

on in airplane?

in the windmill of a minigolf course at night 'cause you think no one is there but then someone comes out, and you quickly try to pretend you are playing golf, but you have no clubs and your pants are around your ankles, so you just look like some kind of mime performance art group and you get arrested and have to pay a fine and are banned from that Putt-Putt forever?

YOU MUST CHOOSE!

Would you rather...

have a three-way with Carrie Underwood and Clay Aiken **OR** Adam Lambert and Kelly Clarkson?

Sarah Palin and John McCain **OR** Barack Obama and Hillary Clinton?

Serena Williams and Venus Williams **OR** Petra Nemcova and Urkel (in character)?

YOU MUST CHOOSE!

Would you rather...

have a threesome with Heidi and Spencer

OR

a brawl with Heidi and Spencer?

Would you... make an agreement with your partner to allow each other 3 celebrities where infidelity would be permitted? If so, who would each of you pick?

YOU MUST CHOOSE!

Would you rather...

have sex with all celebrities whose last names begin with L *OR* W? G *OR* D? C *OR* R?

Would you rather...

come home to find your partner cheating on you

OR

wake up in the middle of the night to find your partner online and masturbating to screen shots of Fozzie Bear?

YOU MUST CHOOSE!

Would you rather...

have a head of long dreadlocks

OR

a crotch of long dreadlock pubes?

Would you rather...

have phone sex with the man who voices AOL's audio prompts

OR

with the man who voices Moviefone?

YOU MUST CHOOSE!

Would you rather have sex with...

this guy   **OR** this guy?

YOU MUST CHOOSE!

Would you rather have sex with...

Amanda Bynes **OR** Stacy Keibler?

Michelle Pfeiffer **OR** Heather Locklear?

Sarah Jessica Parker **OR** Meg Ryan?

Jessica Biel **OR** Katy Perry?

Perez Hilton **OR** Tim Gunn?

Would you rather...

have a total poker face when having an orgasm

OR

speak like an old radio newsman during sex?

Things to consider: (Say in old-time radio voice): The time? 8 p.m. The place? Her tits? The motion? A squeeze.

YOU MUST CHOOSE!

Would you rather...

have nipples that turn green and burst out of your clothing when you get angry

OR

have grappling hook nipples?

Would you rather...

have breast implants of birdseed

OR

breast implants of peanut shells?

YOU MUST CHOOSE!

Would you rather...

your only porn be science books

History Books – Justin Heimberg

Like you haven't pleasured yourself to Harriet Tubman already? Givin' her the old "Underground Railroad?" And Susan B. "Doin' it" Anthony? She's got an ass that won't quit. Not until women's suffrage is achieved, at least. (By the way, can we change the word suffrage to mean something bad? It's confusing.) The point is that there are plenty of historic vixens to smack it to. The tomboy thing that Joan of Arc has going, the erotic mystique of Cleopatra, the eloquent dirty talk of Abigail Adams. It's true what they say: Sometimes we have to look backward to spew forth.

OR history books?

Science Books – David Gomberg

I'll take the vague shape of the female body, organs exposed, over the history book masturbance of a sickly malnourished native Amazonian tribeswoman with diseased saggy breasts dripping to the ground, nipples scraping and tilling the soil. The circulatory system? Hot. Or maybe the pancreas is your thing. One last point: Don't forget that health and sex ed find their way into science books, too. So you can informatively grunt, "I'm gonna ram that labia majoris with the glans of the phallus until I ejaculate my spermatozoa cells!" That's as hot as the specific heat of mercury!

Would You Rather...? Ultimate Sex Edition

Would you rather...

be partially molested by a Yeti (groping, improper talk)

OR

be fully molested by Snuggles the Fabric Softener Bear?

Would you rather...

have pubic hair eyelashes

OR

have no eyelashes?

Things to consider: mascara

YOU MUST CHOOSE!

Would you rather...

when upset, always and exclusively exclaim "Consarnit"

OR

always mutter a low, long, rumbling "Sheeeeeeeyiiiiiiiiiiittttttttttttt"?

Would you rather...

be caught masturbating by your grandfather

OR

vice-versa? Grandmother? Pat Sajak?

YOU MUST CHOOSE!

Would you rather...

have "Total number of sexual partners" be a required box to fill out on every job application

OR

"Average duration of intercourse?"

Would you rather...

have to use condoms two times too big *OR* two times too small?

aluminum foil condoms *OR* the same condom over and over?

condoms covered in sandpaper *OR* condoms covered with pictures of your mother?

YOU MUST CHOOSE!

Would you rather...

have your legal name be Balls Johnson **OR** Stubby McGraw?

Titty Watson **OR** Jackie Taint?

Fritz Nutchap Analbags **OR** Lars Scrotie-scrote Asspacket?

Things to consider: This question paraphrased from Shakespeare's *The Tempest*

YOU MUST CHOOSE!

Would you rather...

be a world class sprinter but only when fully erect

OR

be a world class swimmer but only while naked?

Things to consider: pelvic thrusting at the finish line

Would you rather...

have your nipples dipped in liquid nitrogen and shattered

OR

your earlobes clipped off with garden hedgers?

YOU MUST CHOOSE!

Would you rather have phone sex with...

Bill O'Reilly **OR** T-Pain with autotune?

William Faulkner **OR** Kermit the Frog?

Nelson Mandela and Sienna Miller (on conference) **OR** Anna Kournikova and Ozzy Osbourne?

YOU MUST CHOOSE!

Would you rather have phone sex with...

Celine Dion **OR** Maya Angelou?

a severely congested Alyssa Milano **OR** Soledad O'Brien?

Penelope Cruz and Larry Bird (on conference) **OR** Ariana Huffington and World Wrestling Entertainment's Jim Ross?

Things to consider: misunderstandings due to accents, arm-drag take-downs

YOU MUST CHOOSE!

Would you rather...

dive through a Slip-N-Slide covered in sheep excrement and urine

OR

get a Mentos and Diet Coke enema?

Would you rather...

draw your dating pool from people browsing the Self Help section of the book store

OR

the Sci-Fi section?

YOU MUST CHOOSE!

Would you rather...

see an opera based on your love life

OR

a porno based on your sex life?

Would you rather...

always orgasm thirty seconds into sex

OR

only be able to orgasm after three hours of continuous sex?

YOU MUST CHOOSE!

Would you rather...

have breast implants made of Nerf **OR** Play-Doh?

quarters **OR** thumb tacks?

coffee grounds **OR** Pillsbury Doughboys?

tadpoles **OR** helium?

Things to consider: babies' high-pitched cries after breast-feeding, frog maturation

YOU MUST CHOOSE!

Would you rather...

your genitalia was located on the palm of your hand

Neck – Justin Heimberg

One word. Ascot. It can just be kind of your thing. With neckitals®, you can combine the ecstasy of eating with the ecstasy of sex—if you swallow just right, applying gentle pressure to the underside of the neck, you can stimulate your g-spot. If your junk was on your hands, be you a woman or man, you'd have to always explain why you are wearing that one mitten and why you aren't applauding after a show; or worse, you will applaud, hurting or arousing yourself with each clap until your mitten gets soiled. Plus, through rigorous sex, one of your arms would become way more muscular than the other, making you grotesquely asymmetrical (as if having hand genitals wasn't bad enough.)

OR the front of your neck?

Hand it over – David Gomberg

Imagine sex. On your hand, you have all kinds of maneuverability. With neck-nuts, you're relegated to lying down and letting someone ride or thrust against you until you can't breathe. And yes, you can hide your hand genitals with a mitten and learn to write with the other hand. But neck balls, those are tough to hide (as is neck labia.) In fact being a woman is particularly distasteful in that with each intercourse thrust, you're getting a mouthful of mantuft.™ And you won't develop asymmetrical muscles, because, on one hand (literally), you have the goods to have sex with; and on the other hand, literally sort of, you'd be using it to stimulate yourself during self-pleasure. Yin and yang. The balance of life.

Would you rather...

use used Kleenex to wipe your ass

OR

use used toilet paper to blow your nose?

Would you rather...

have your parents walk in on you while you are having sex

OR

walk in on them?

YOU MUST CHOOSE!

Would you rather...

have asparagus for nipples

OR

pipe cleaners for pubic hair?

Would you rather...

marry the spouse of your dreams but gain 10 pounds a year

OR

have him or her gain 10 pounds a year?

YOU MUST CHOOSE!

Would you rather...

have a lover who is 6'3" tall with 3-inch penis **OR** 5'2" tall with a 9-inch penis?

7' tall with a 1-inch penis **OR** 2' tall with a 12-inch penis?

18' tall with a 4-inch penis **OR** 1' tall with a 64-inch penis?

Would you rather...

have your ears and nipples switch places

OR

your nose and genitals?

Things to consider: cutting ear holes in sweaters, foreplay

YOU MUST CHOOSE!

You live with a roommate. You decide to use a blacklight to check your room for hidden "stains."

Would you rather find stains all over...

your washcloth **OR** your favorite cereal bowl?

your computer keyboard and mouse **OR** a framed photo of your family?

a copy of George Washington Carver's autobiography **OR** a copy of *Would You Rather...? Ultimate Sex Edition*?

YOU MUST CHOOSE!

Would you rather only be able to have sex while playing...

"Eye of the Tiger" **OR** "Hava Nagila"?

Buffalo Springfield's "For What It's Worth" **OR** "Beethoven's Ninth Symphony"?

"Pants on the Ground" **OR** William Hung's rendition of "She Bangs"?

the *Star Trek* theme **OR** the *Schindler's List* theme?

an audio book of *Angela's Ashes* **OR** recordings of a senile man trying to find his way out of a K-Mart?

YOU MUST CHOOSE!

Would you rather your only porn be...

6-second clips of hot people **OR** 2-minute clips of moderately attractive people?

verbose, subtle erotic fiction **OR** pornographic Magic Eye 3D pictures (the ones where you have to stare just right until the image comes into focus)?

Spanish channel variety shows **OR** vague, slightly inaccurate recollections of a 1980's Markie Post?

animal nature documentaries **OR** suggestive cloud formations?

geometric shapes **OR** family reunion pictures?

Things to consider: the arousing rhombus

YOU MUST CHOOSE!

Would you rather...

eat a pubic hair cotton candy

OR

a fecal chili dog?

Would you rather...

watch _____ have sex
(insert two unattractive acquaintances)

OR

get a lap dance by _____ ?
(insert friend's parent)

YOU MUST CHOOSE!

Would you rather have sex with...

just the top half of Jessica Alba

OR

just the bottom half of Jessica Alba?

Would you rather...

have a sexual partner who has a lettuce fetish

OR

a foot-measuring device fetish?

YOU MUST CHOOSE!

Would you rather...

go to a dentist with Parkinson's

OR

a proctologist with Parkinson's?

Would you rather...

have a penis that sheds skin like a snake every week

OR

a penis that makes the sound of a rainstick when it moves?

YOU MUST CHOOSE!

Would you rather...

have to eat like a baby bird where your mom regurgitates partially digested food into your mouth

OR

only be able to eat food that has been partially digested and excreted by some living thing?

Would you rather...

find a condom at the bottom of your vanilla milkshake

OR

sip a bowl of gazpacho only to discover a pubic hair at the bottom?

YOU MUST CHOOSE!

Would you rather...

HAVE COMMERCIAL INTERRUPTIONS DURING MASTURBATION FANTASIES

HAVE TO MASTURBATE WITH THE MANDATORY USE OF AN ELMO HAND PUPPET?

Would you rather...

grope _____
(insert hot person)

or

have sex with _____ ?
(insert average looking person)

Would you rather...

fart wetly and loudly in front of _____
(insert relative)

or

_____ ?
(insert someone you have a crush on or are trying to impress)

YOU MUST CHOOSE!

Would you rather...

take off your clothes, squat, and make a number two
in front of _____
(insert friend's parents)

OR

put a mask on, sneak up, and put a sleeper hold on

_____ ?
(insert friend's mom)

Would you rather...

have your genitals located on your _____
(insert body part)

OR

your _____ ?
(insert another body part)

YOU MUST CHOOSE!

Would you rather...

have to mutually masturbate with _____
(insert inappropriate acquaintance)

OR

go down on _____ ?
(insert unhygienic person)

Would you rather...

manually stimulate _____
(insert close friend's father)

OR

have a three-way with _____
(insert close friend's parents)

while _____ watched?
(insert the ghost of a historical figure)

YOU MUST CHOOSE!

Would you rather...

have nightly sex with _____ for a week
<small>(insert unattractive person)</small>

OR

for the same week, be the official "wiper" of

_____ ?
<small>(insert person you know with bad stomach issues)</small>

Would you... sit in the bleachers and heckle the outfielders at a Special Olympics softball game for an inning for $13,000?

YOU MUST CHOOSE!

Would you... masturbate only to *National Geographic* for the rest of your life for $500,000?

Would you... take the surname of your spouse upon marriage (they were adamant about it) if it were "Chode"? "Doodition"? Cheeksqueakers?"

Would you rather...

have your love emails posted on Google's home page

OR

have your sex dreams available via Netflix DVD?

YOU MUST CHOOSE!

Would you rather have sex with...

this guy OR this guy?

YOU MUST CHOOSE!

Would you... if the Deity made it possible, have a third nipple for $100,000? At 100,000 a nipple, how many would you have?

Would you... want to have sex with Megan Fox if she gained 50 pounds? 80? 100? 200?

Would you... want to have sex with Johnny Depp if he gained 50 pounds? 100? 200?

YOU MUST CHOOSE!

Would you... have sex with Leonardo DiCaprio (women)/Shakira (men) if he/she had no teeth? No teeth and no hair? No teeth, no hair, no knees, and an incurable case of the hiccups?

Would you... put your penis in a glory hole for $60,000 if you were told there was an equal chance of your mother, Jenna Jameson, and Greg Gumbel being on the other side?

YOU MUST CHOOSE!

Which of the following would you have sex with... for your choice of $200,000 or the chance to have sex with your top five celebrities?

a sheep?

a cow?

an armadillo?

a rhino?

Will Purdue?

a baboon?

a beehive?

YOU MUST CHOOSE!

Would you... watch a porno movie starring your parents for $1,000? $10,000? $100,000? What's your price?

Would you... watch a porno movie with your parents for $1,000? $10,000? $100,000?

Would you... have sex with a creature that was half Marissa Miller/half horse? Which half would you want as the lower half and which as the upper?

YOU MUST CHOOSE!

If your life depended on it, would you rather...

have to achieve orgasm while listening to Al Gore give a long boring speech about climate change

OR

while staring at a framed 8x10 photo of former surgeon general C. Everett Koop?

Things to consider: Try it. You have five minutes.

YOU MUST CHOOSE!

Would you rather...

have a permanent smile

OR

a permanent erection?

Things to consider: church, visiting grandma, funerals

Would you slyly masturbate to the point of orgasm...

on a public bus for $5,000?

at a Quiznos for $7,000?

at your desk at work during working hours for $10,000?

at church for $200,000?

YOU MUST CHOOSE!

If your life depended on it, would you rather have to have sex to the point of orgasm...

while staying on a running treadmill **OR** staying on a unicycle without falling off?

on a pogo stick **OR** on a seesaw without either end hitting the ground?

on an exercise ball without falling off **OR** sitting on a George Foreman Grill enduring the pain?

YOU MUST CHOOSE!

Would you rather...

have bland, unspectacular sex with Antonio Banderas

OR

wild, passionate, freaky sex with Bryant Gumbel?

Would you rather...

have bland, unspectacular sex with Jessica Biel

OR

wild, passionate, freaky sex with Condoleezza Rice?

YOU MUST CHOOSE!

Would you rather...

when getting too into it during sex, "tilt" like a pinball machine and stop functioning for a while

OR

be transported to Des Moines every time you orgasm?

Would you rather...

watch a stripper who visibly suffers from severe arthritis *OR* who is stricken with problem flatulence?

who is 60 pounds overweight *OR* who dances with a Hitler theme?

with protruding varicose veins *OR* who eerily resembles Tommy Lasorda?

YOU MUST CHOOSE!

Would you rather...

have to wear noise-proof headphones during sex

OR

a full leg cast?

Would you rather...

have sex with someone with horrible bacne

OR

with someone who has a life-size portrait tattoo
of your uncle on their back?

YOU MUST CHOOSE!

Would you rather...

have to talk during sex in baby talk

OR

in beatnik slang from the '50s?

Would you rather...

have your Facebook status update automatically and report all specific sexual activity, down to the last detail, in real time

OR

have your Facebook profile display a complete group of people you've hooked up with?

YOU MUST CHOOSE!

Would you rather...

have a threesome with Colin Farrell and Artie Lang

OR

Matt Lauer and Bob Sagat?

Would you rather...

have a threesome with Gisele Bundchen
and Rosie O'Donnell

OR

with two average looking women?

YOU MUST CHOOSE!

Would you rather...

have sex in an airplane bathroom

OR

on a golf course at night?

Would you rather...

only be able to have sex missionary *OR* doggie-style?

oral sex *OR* intercourse?

performing a 69 *OR* a 37?

YOU MUST CHOOSE!

Would you rather use as a sex toy...

a menorah **OR** a shoehorn?

a backscratcher **OR** a Rubik's Snake?

a wacky wall-walker **OR** a Swiffer?

Would you rather...

have sex with Pinocchio

OR

with your choice of Snow White's dwarves?

YOU MUST CHOOSE!

Would you rather...

be a supervillain that can kill people's sex drive at any moment with the perfect personalized mood-killing hologram

OR

a supervillain who can queef 4.5 Richter scale earthquakes?

Would you rather...

speak like a pirate during sex

OR

yodel upon orgasm?

YOU MUST CHOOSE!

If your life depended on it, would you rather...

have to bring yourself to orgasm while your mom leaves you a long rambling answering machine message

OR

while staring, eyelids held open, at a poster of an adorable kitten?

Would you rather...

have porn-quality sex but porn-quality conversation as well

OR

have romantic-comedy-quality sex and romantic-comedy-quality conversation?

Would you rather...

all of your drunken phone calls be recorded and played back on a popular radio station

OR

have all your love letters read dramatically by William Shatner on a TV special?

YOU MUST CHOOSE!

Three-ways with Celebrity Supercouple Fish

Would you rather have a three-way with...

Albacore (Jessica Alba and Corey Feldman) **OR** Katfish (Kat Von D and Laurence Fishburne)?

Sardean (Sarah Michelle Gellar and Dean Cain) **OR** Halibut (Halle Berry and Boutros Boutros-Ghali – alternative name Boutros Boutros Halle)?

Moray (Demi Moore and Ray Liota) **OR** Portmanteau (Natalie Portman and Tony Danza)?

YOU MUST CHOOSE!

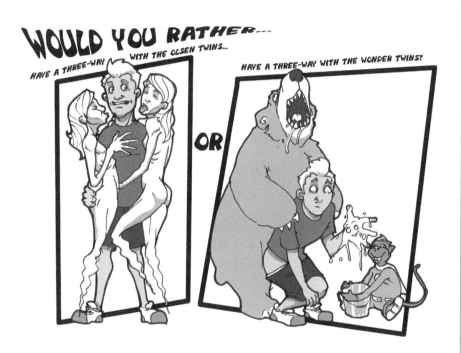

Would you rather...

watch your parents having sex

OR

watch your grandparents having sex?

Would you... have sex with a 70-year-old

Marlon Brando to have sex with a 30-year-old Marlon Brando?

YOU MUST CHOOSE!

Would you... have sex with a walrus to have sex with all the Playmates of the current year (men); with *People*'s 50 Sexiest Men Alive (women)?

Would you... have sex with Tyne Daly daily, to have sex with Keira Knightly, nightly?

YOU MUST CHOOSE!

Would you rather...

be unable to shake the sporadic image of Gene Shalit during sexual congress

OR

have pubic hair that grows whenever you're lying?

Would you rather...

have crab claws for nipples

OR

have a unique venereal disease where anytime you kiss someone you briefly turn into an 1800's gold prospector, who is dead-set on the finding that next big strike?

YOU MUST CHOOSE!

Would you rather...

be unable to perform sexually unless dressed up
as a Spanish Conquistador

OR

when attempting to shout out your partner's name
when having sex, always instead yell "Stombin 6!"?

Would you rather...

have to wear foam "Number 1" hands when having sex

OR

have to wear loafers without socks?

YOU MUST CHOOSE!

Would you rather...

have sex with Danny DeVito

OR

Orville Redenbacher?

Would you rather...

have genitalia that permanently reduces in size
by a millimeter each time it is used

OR

genitalia that multiplies after ten uses?

YOU MUST CHOOSE!

Would you rather...

have your libido vary directly with the stock market

OR

have the sexual outcome of your dates be contingent on what base you reach, if any, via a roll of dice in Strat-O-Matic baseball?

Would you rather...

have one of your sexual encounters webcast

OR

appear in a Zagat-style guide based on submissions from your various sexual partners?

Things to consider: a "bumbling novice" who "couldn't find a clitoris with a divining rod" offers "mildly pleasant groping" and is "over in a flash."

YOU MUST CHOOSE!

Pick Your Penis

Would you rather...

have a penis that beeped like a Geiger counter the closer you get to a partner willing to put out **OR** have a penis that dispensed freshly brewed coffee?

have a penis the consistency of bamboo **OR** the consistency of one of those water-filled things—I think it was called a snake—y'know, that rubber thing... you'd like squeeze it, and it'd squirm? That thing! From the '80s, you know what I'm talking about?

YOU MUST CHOOSE!

Would you rather...

have to have sex through a hole in a sheet

OR

through a hole in a bagel?

Would you rather...

only be able to sleep with sexual partners over the height of 7 feet tall **OR** under the height of 4 feet?

partners weighing over 500 pounds **OR** under 70 pounds?

partners whose names have exactly 11 letters **OR** partners with cool scars?

YOU MUST CHOOSE!

Fun with Scrotums

Would you... dunk your scrotal sack in a pot of boiling water for ten seconds for $50,000?

Would you rather...

have a scrotum that inflates and deflates like a bullfrog's throat

OR

a scrotum that hangs all the way to the ground?

YOU MUST CHOOSE!

Would you rather...

be completely incapable of moving when sexually attracted to someone

OR

mentally revert to yourself as a 4-year-old whenever you are about to have any sort of sexual contact?

During sex, would you rather a woman say...

"I love you!" *OR* "F**k that pussy!"?

"You're the greatest!" *OR* "Give it to me!"?

"Crack my toes!" *OR* "The overlord shall be pleased!"?

YOU MUST CHOOSE!

Would you rather...

have your dirty talk dubbed with clean sound-alike words
(eg. "Fork that pony!"; "Sick that dog!")

OR

your dirty talk come out in sped-up "chipmunk speak"?

Would you rather...

have phone sex *OR* cybersex?

charades sex *OR* Pictionary sex?

snail mail sex *OR* doing that thing where you put your
hands together and you interlock fingers with someone and
you open it and it's like a vagina, or maybe a butthole?

YOU MUST CHOOSE!

Would you rather...

URINATE THROUGH
YOUR NOSE

OR

SMELL THINGS WITH
YOUR GENITALIA?

Would you rather have sex with...

Javier Bardem **OR** Christian Bale?

Jon Stewart **OR** Stephen Colbert?

Adam Brody **OR** Michael Cera?

Nick Carter **OR** Aaron Carter?

a Teenage Mutant Ninja Turtle **OR** Mike Huckabee?

YOU MUST CHOOSE!

Would you rather...

be the world's greatest lover but marry your high school sweetheart at age 18

OR

have the talents of Shakespeare but be restricted to writing for *Penthouse Forum*?

Would you rather...

like big butts and be unable to fabricate about such matters

OR

find out your girlfriend is a centerfold, causing your blood temperature to starkly plummet?

YOU MUST CHOOSE!

Would you rather...

have sex with Kathy Griffin on a waterbed

OR

with Megan Fox on a bed of rusty nails?

Would you rather...

have action figures made from your various sexual partners

OR

have Ken Burns make a nine part documentary about your sex life?

Would you rather...

always be drunk during sex

OR

never be drunk during sex?

YOU MUST CHOOSE!

Would you rather...

have sex on bed sheets depicting bloody scenes from wars

OR

sheets with smiling pictures of your parents?

Would you rather...

have to list your penis size/breast size on your business card

OR

have to use the email address for all business and pleasure: hobbitpumper@gmail.com?

YOU MUST CHOOSE!

Would you rather...

have an ass crack that is 2/3 the way to the left of your body

OR

have an ass crack that extends up to in between your shoulder blades?

Would you rather...

only be able to communicate during romance and sex through facial expression

OR

text message?

YOU MUST CHOOSE!

Would you rather...

bump, grind, freak, and otherwise dirty dance with

_____

(insert friend's mom or teacher or someone else inappropriate)

OR

pose naked for _____ ?

(insert magazine)

Would you rather...

have a threesome with _____

(insert attractive acquaintance)

and _____

(insert unattractive acquaintance)

OR

have a threesome with _____ ?

(insert two average looking acquaintances)

YOU MUST CHOOSE!

Would you rather...

have a RealDoll of _____

(insert someone you know)

OR

a Voodoo doll of _____ ?

(insert someone you dislike)

Would you rather have sex with...

Brad Pitt if he gained 60 pounds all in the gut **OR** Jonah Hill?

a gap-toothed Matt Damon **OR** Chris Parnell?

Louie Anderson **OR** a racist-remark-spouting Tom Brady?

YOU MUST CHOOSE!

Would you rather...

WATCH A PORNO MOVIE WITH YOUR PARENTS

OR

WATCH A PORNO MOVIE STARRING YOUR PARENTS?

Would you rather...

watch a porno with your parents

With your parents – Justin Heimberg

No amount of awkwardness could possibly outweigh the agonizing disgust of watching the undulating naked bodies of your parents. There are secrets that must be kept. Things that must remain hidden. Seeing your parents banging is akin to unlocking the Ark in *Raiders of the Lost Ark*. Your head will shrivel, your face will melt. It is Pandora's box opened along with your mother's. It is a no-win situation. If they are slow and inept at making love, it is pathetic and painful, but if they are fast and furious and skilled, well then that image is a vision of hell I wish upon no one.

OR watch a porno *starring* your parents?

Starring your parents – David Gomberg

I know I take the less popular position here, but hear me
out. The experience of watching your parents have sex, while
gross and unholy, is a private one. It is a shame that one can
pack away and repress, and though you may never view your
parents again without imagining them with their clothes
off, they at least, are none the wiser. But if you watch
something obscene together, that will always stand between
you—that fifteen minutes of squirming discomfort. If you've
ever watched a borderline dirty moment on TV with your
parents and felt that pang of awkwardness, multiply that
by 1000, and you'll know what you would feel.

"Would you rather...?"
Questions you can test!

Much of what we write is very "Do not try this at home." But here are some perfectly healthy ideas when tried in the safety and privacy of your own home.

When receiving cunnilingus, would you rather have the man use his tongue to spell out...

the cursive English alphabet **OR** non-cursive capital letters?

the phrase "I am the greatest" **OR** "Milton is incorrigible"?

the Hebrew alphabet **OR** the alphabet by tapping it out in Morse code?

YOU MUST CHOOSE!

Would you rather...

be eating a salad and find a long, long hair in your mouth

OR

lick a Tootsie Pop, only to find a small human embryo in the middle?

Would you rather...

sleep nightly in pajamas made of used dental gauze

OR

have to reach into a horse's ass every time you want the key to your apartment?

YOU MUST CHOOSE!

Would you rather...

use a cheese grater to grate off five back moles

OR

wipe yourself with extra-adhesive tape?

Would you rather...

have to keep a hard-boiled egg in your mouth for a day

OR

have to keep it in your ass for a day?

YOU MUST CHOOSE!

Would you rather...

defecate colorful and intricate kaleidoscope patterns

OR

urinate in solid rods?

Would you rather...

breathe through your navel

OR

your butt?

Things to consider: snorkeling

YOU MUST CHOOSE!

Would you rather...

have Internet chat sex (including video of faces but with no volume) with someone who is hot as hell but is just an egregiously awful speller

OR

someone who is decent looking and has great writing panache and grammar skills?

Things to consider: I wunt to nale you. I am masterbating to a clymacks. Are you into annul?

Would you rather...

have sex with someone who has the butt
of Kim Kardashian and the face of Kim Jong Il

OR

the body of Halle Berry and the head
of Franken Berry?

YOU MUST CHOOSE!

Would you rather...

have nipples that made the sound of a doorbell when pressed

OR

an ass that made the sound of a foghorn when squeezed?

Would you rather...

have a speech impediment where you switch "f" sounds and "d" sounds

OR

where you switch "c" sounds and "r" sounds?

Things to consider: feeding the ducks, the runt of the litter, playing darts, rock-hard abs, etc.

YOU MUST CHOOSE!

Would you rather...

shadowbox in your sleep

OR

have a penis that, when erect, points to the correct time like the hour hand on a clock?

Things to consider: sleeping next to someone, difficulty of having a sexual relationship, breaking nightstand lamps, 3:30

Would you rather...

take 900 consecutive punches to the taint by Chuck Norris

OR

have your eyelids pulled taut and cut off by tweezers?

Things to consider: likelihood of survival after taint pummeling, sleeping, bloody tears (for both options), literally having the shit beat out of you

YOU MUST CHOOSE!

Would you rather...

have sex with the first human image you see when you Google "pelican enthusiast"

OR

the first human image you see when you Google "milky thighs"?

Would you rather...

sneeze inward

OR

fart inward?

YOU MUST CHOOSE!

Would you rather...

have diarrhea of the mouth, literally

OR

have a stick up your ass, literally?

Would you rather...

stutter at the end of every word-d-d-d

OR

have written *fuck!* Tourette's Syndrome *balls!*?

Things to *ass-munch!* consider: power point *dildo!* presentations, love letters *cunttrap!*; *shit-ass!*; *fuck!*; *dickdangle!*

YOU MUST CHOOSE!

Would you rather have...

five 2-inch penises located in your general crotch area

OR

three 4-inch penises, with one located on your knee, one on the small of your back, and one branching from the aforementioned penis that is on your knee?

Things to consider: dual input ability, orgies, hurrying like a plate spinner to achieve multiple orgasm

Would you rather...

have no joints

OR

thirteen anuses?

Things to consider: defecating would resemble Whack-a-mole

YOU MUST CHOOSE!

Would you rather...

have sex with Nicole Richie if she gained 75 pounds

OR

lost 25 pounds?

Would you rather...

your Lamaze coach be that excitable Spanish
soccer announcer

OR

Jesse Jackson?

YOU MUST CHOOSE!

Would you rather...

have sex with Johnny Depp if he put on 75 pounds

OR

George Clooney if he gained 75 pounds?

Things to consider: Who'd carry the weight better?

Would you rather...

have a sexual partner who talks to you like a motivational speaker during sex

OR

that talks to you like a "bad cop" interrogator?

YOU MUST CHOOSE!

Would you rather have sex with...

Taylor Swift **OR** Jennifer Garner?

Anna Faris **OR** *Top Chef*'s Padma Lakshmi?

Things to consider: Salman Rushdie tapped that.

Crazy, chunky Britney circa 2008 **OR** sane, nubile Britney circa 2003?

Paula Abdul **OR** Megan Fox if she were missing an arm? A leg? An eye? Missing all of the above?

YOU MUST CHOOSE!

Would you rather have sex with...

Donald Trump **OR** Vince McMahon?

Topher Grace **OR** LeBron James?

Seth Rogen **OR** Mario Lopez?

Dennis Kucinich if he had a 10-inch penis **OR**
John Edwards if he had a 3-inch penis?

YOU MUST CHOOSE!

Would you rather...

get to second base with Jessica Simpson

OR

go all the way with Tara Reid?

Would you rather...

get to first base with Angelina Jolie

OR

third base with Helen Hunt?

Would you rather...

get hit by a pitch with Monica Bellucci

OR

foul off a couple close ones and then strike out looking with Briana Banks?

YOU MUST CHOOSE!

Would you rather...

have access to a MySpace-like online community where it was revealed who everyone has had sex with and who their partners have had sex with, and so on

OR

have a TiVo that magically records everything that goes through your partner's head during sex?

YOU MUST CHOOSE!

Would you rather...

have a Jenna Jameson vaginal replica

OR

a RealDoll crafted in the spitting image of Louisa May Alcott?

YOU MUST CHOOSE!

Would you rather...

live like Bonobo monkeys (who have feverish 30-second bouts of sex every five minutes, all in the midst of carrying out their daily activities)

OR

have sex like rhinos who charge into each other for hours before determining if a mate is worthy, followed by an hour and a half of sex where a male can ejaculate up to ten times?

YOU MUST CHOOSE!

Would you... dry-hump a koala bear for a complete understanding of badminton strategy?

Would you... spend two weeks wearing nothing but a g-string and Tivas for $15,000?

Would you... give up 2 years of your life to have a penis that was 3 inches longer (men) or breasts that were 3 sizes larger (women)?

YOU MUST CHOOSE!

Which are real names for deviant sexual maneuvers and which are fake?

Arabian Goggles (testicles settle in eye sockets)

Viking Funeral (a woman's manual stimulation of two phalluses above her head)

Cleveland Steamer (feces is laid upon chest for erotic purposes)

A Poor Man's Walrus (double nasal penetration)

Answers: Arabian Goggles and Cleveland Steamer are real.

YOU MUST CHOOSE!

Would you rather...

have to drive with only your nondominant hand for the rest of your life

OR

have to pleasure yourself only with your nondominant hand?

YOU MUST CHOOSE!

Note: The following question has been paraphrased from Immanuel Kant's *Groundwork of the Metaphysics of Morals*.

Would you rather...

have your feces undulate and ooze like in a lava lamp upon falling in the toilet

OR

be able to fart Morse code?

Things to consider: rainy days; secretly relaying the truth if captured and filmed by terrorists

YOU MUST CHOOSE!

Would you rather...

BE COMPELLED TO ENTER EVERY ROOM BY JUMPING INTO THE DOORWAY WITH AN IMAGINARY PISTOL LIKE THE STAR OF A 70'S COP SHOW

OR

INVARIABLY MAKE YOUR ORGASM FACE INSTEAD OF SMILING WHEN BEING PHOTOGRAPHED?

Would you rather...

have breasts and a butt that age ten times faster
than the rest of your body

OR

have your neck and feet age ten times faster
than the rest of your body?

Would you rather...

drink a cappuccino topped with whipped, rabid-St. Bernard
slobber froth

OR

iced tea sweetened with a spoonful of vaginal discharge
from a VH1's *Rock of Love* with Bret Michaels contestant?

Things to consider: getting infected

YOU MUST CHOOSE!

Would you rather...

have your genitalia located on the back of your left hand **OR** the back of your neck?

on the middle of your back **OR** on your elbow?

on your hip **OR** your ankle?

Things to consider: oral sex, masturbation, tailoring bills

Would you rather...

eat a jelly doughnut full of snot

OR

a Danish iced with yak semen?

YOU MUST CHOOSE!

Would you rather...

your photo was used on a herpes medication billboard

OR

for an ad for an impotence drug?

Would you rather...

have masturbated to Internet porn only to realize you left on the Skype video conference with your mom

OR

find out there has been a hidden camera in your shower for the past year?

YOU MUST CHOOSE!

Would you rather...

throw up in zero gravity

OR

have diarrhea in zero gravity?

Would you rather...

watch your grandparents' sloppy make-out/grope session

OR

discover they are watching yours lasciviously?

YOU MUST CHOOSE!

Would you rather...

brush your teeth nightly for six months with a copious inch-long portion of smegma

OR

use a used tampon to brew a mug of tea?

Would you rather...

have a neurological abnormality that causes you to, after sex, appeal victoriously to an imaginary crowd à la Hulk Hogan

OR

have a condition where as soon as you see someone take their clothes off, you point to the "appropriate" body parts and say quite suavely, "milk, milk, lemonade, 'round the corner fudge is made"?

YOU MUST CHOOSE!

Would you rather...

every hour on the hour, change which gender you are attracted to

OR

turn your sexual partner into Tony Danza when you climax, and then turn them back to themselves the next time you have sex with them?

Things to consider: maintaining a marriage, determining who the boss is

Would you rather...

utter all exclamations during sex in Yiddish *OR* Chinese?

in sign language *OR* in the form of a question as if on *Jeopardy*?

in Pig Latin *OR* with IM acronyms?

Things to consider: abgray atthay itttaytay; lol, ftp, diitbh, ccr, elo, bto

YOU MUST CHOOSE!

Would you rather...

ejaculate a deadly dart

OR

die if you are not having sex at 3:37 pm every day?

Things to consider: moving to Vegas, pulling out, work as a spy

Would you... have sex with someone of the opposite sex who has a perfect body, but has your face?

YOU MUST CHOOSE!

Would you rather...

everything you say be considered an insult

OR

a come-on?

Would you rather...

have horrible camel toe, no matter what you wear

OR

have nipple-itis (constant visibly erect nipples that show through anything you wear)?

Things to considers: tuxedoes, the beach, short shorts

YOU MUST CHOOSE!

Would you rather have sex with...

this guy

OR this guy?

Would you rather your only means of birth control be...

gum **OR** an English muffin?

a rubber band and a box of Tic Tacs **OR** a roll of "Jazz Icon" postage stamps?

a waffle cone **OR** anal sex?

a stapler **OR** an 8"x10" photograph of Wilfred Brimley?

YOU MUST CHOOSE!

MOOD MUSIC

The Deity is going to help you set the mood with something from his private music collection.

Would you rather...

always have to have sex to Arab prayer music **OR** ragtime music?

"Oklahoma" **OR** "Swing Low, Sweet Chariot?"

The Lone Ranger theme **OR** "Wipeout?"

"99 Red Balloons" **OR** "99 Luftballons?"

vocabulary builder CD's **OR** a loop of Louis Gossett, Jr. coughing?

YOU MUST CHOOSE!

Would you rather have sex with...

Da Vinci's "Mona Lisa"

YOU MUST CHOOSE!

OR Picasso's "Woman with Fan"?

YOU MUST CHOOSE!

Would you rather...

have orgasms that feel like a brain-freeze

OR

be able to maintain an erection (men)/reach orgasm (women) only by accurately reciting the digits of Pi (you have to start over if you mess up)?

Things to consider: 3.141592653589793238462643383279502884197 16939937510582097494459230781640628620899862803482534211 70679821480865132823066470938446095505822317253594081284 81117450284102701938521105559644622948954930381964428810 9 75665933446128475648233786783165271201909145648566923460 34861045432664821339360726024914127372458700660631558817 4 88152092096282925409171536436789259003...

YOU MUST CHOOSE!

Pick your penis!

Would you rather have...

(women, read the following questions as "have a partner with")

a 4-inch long penis with a 2-inch diameter **OR** an 8-inch penis with a half-inch diameter?

an 8-inch penis that was always soft **OR** a 3-inch penis that was always hard?

a retractable penis **OR** a detachable penis?

a penis able to drink like an elephant uses his trunk **OR** a penis that glows in the dark when you twist the head?

YOU MUST CHOOSE!

Game: Face off

Whoever is reading must convey the words by using only their head and face. Everything below the neck must remain still.

Cunnilingus

Deepthroat

Constipation

Orgasm

Bukkake

Jack Nicholson

Fart

YOU MUST CHOOSE!

Would you rather have...

(women, read the following questions as "have a partner with")

a two-pronged penis **OR** a right angle penis?

a penis that turns green and tears out of your clothing like the Incredible Hulk every time you get aroused **OR** an invisible penis?

a Black & Decker Flex Light penis **OR** a penis that can act as a light saber upon your command?

five penises **OR** one big penis and one small penis?

Things to consider: clitoral stimulation; with five penises, your pants fit like a glove; with one big and one small, your pants fit like a mitten

YOU MUST CHOOSE!

Would you rather...

ejaculate guacamole **OR** Tabasco sauce?

Scope **OR** crazy string?

air-rifle bb's **OR** high voltage electric shocks?

Bee Gee's music **OR** baseball umpire strike and ball calls?

through your nostrils **OR** through your eyes?

Would you rather have sex with...

Russell Crowe **OR** Pierce Brosnan?

Gerard Butler **OR** James Franco?

Clay Aiken **OR** Ruben Studdard?

YOU MUST CHOOSE!

Would you rather have sex with...

Gwen Stefani **OR** Jennifer Aniston?

Eliza Dushku **OR** Jennifer Love Hewitt?

the new Daisy Duke (Jessica Simpson) **OR**
Classic Daisy Duke (Catherine Bach)?

Rebecca Romijn **OR** Rebecca Romijn-Stamos?

YOU MUST CHOOSE!

Would you rather have phone sex with...

Dr. Seuss **OR** Dr. House (in character)?

Hardball's Chris Matthews **OR** Donald Trump?

Alf **OR** Bob Ross (the calm "Happy Trees" painter from PBS)?

Marcel Marceau **OR** Rush Limbaugh?

YOU MUST CHOOSE!

Would you rather have phone sex with...

Oprah **OR** Martha Stewart?

Barbara Bush **OR** Hillary Clinton?
Things to consider: Barbara Bush has a mouth like a sailor

Margaret Cho **OR** the ghost of Harriet Tubman?

someone who constantly corrects your grammar **OR**
someone prone to quoting Joseph Goebbels throughout?

Gary Gnu **OR** Pegasus?

Would you rather...

have a mountain range named after you

OR

have a sexual position officially named
after you?

YOU MUST CHOOSE!

Would you rather...

HAVE SEX WITH A GUY THAT HAS THE BODY OF JOHN GOODMAN AND THE FACE OF BRAD PITT

OR

THE BODY OF BRAD PITT AND THE FACE OF MAYOR MCCHEESE?

Would you rather...

have sex with a woman that has the body of Janet Reno and the face of Angelina Jolie

OR

the body of Angelina Jolie and the face of former Milwaukee Buck Jack Sikma?

Things to consider: doggie-style

YOU MUST CHOOSE!

Immoral Dilemmas

Since the beginning of eternity, the Deity has always been fascinated by humankind's capacity for right and wrong. He impishly delights in the vicarious struggles of conscience ping-ponging during a mortal's decision-making process. And so he poses to you these questions of conscience.

An unbelievably attractive spouse of a close friend offers you the chance for a one-time "no one will know" affair. Do you partake in oral or anal sex?

You are walking down the street when you see someone drop a hundred dollar bill and walk off obliviously. Do you spend the money on meth or crack?

You hear a woman screaming as if being attacked in the parking lot behind your apartment building. Do you watch *The Office* or *CSI*?

You're attractive, but poor and without skills. Someone offers you lot of money to work for an escort service. How can I get in touch with you?

The teacher asks if you wrote your son's book report. Your son claimed he did it, but the teacher's right. Do you concentrate on defending the report's racism or anti-Semitism?

You're buying a house from an old lady. She's asking a price that is way too low. Do you partake in oral or anal sex?

Paper or plastic?

A social agency wants to establish a residence for seven retarded adults next door to your house. Another neighbor has written up a petition against the home and asks you to sign. Do you dominate the retards in basketball or football?

Your father is having an affair and your mother is unaware of it. High five or fist bump?

Venti or Grande?

It's Thursday, and you are raping an antelope.
Do you wear a Nixon mask?

You remarry and find that your new spouse is allergic to the dog you've had for eight years. Who do you put down first?

It's 4 a.m. and you are stopped at a red light on a country road that seems like it's never going to change. No one is in sight. Do you masturbate with your left or right hand?

Democrat or Republican?

You're in your hometown and you bump into your old girlfriend. With your penis. Over and over. Such is life.

Would you rather...

get sexually turned on by hearing increasingly difficult *Jeopardy!* questions

OR

be turned on by dirty talk spoken in the style of a Cockney British chimney sweep?

Would you rather...

have your sexual fantasies edited in your mind for appropriate television viewing

OR

have the *Reading Rainbow* guy appear and tell you the moral at the end of every masturbation fantasy?

Things to consider: passionate kissing, implied intercourse

YOU MUST CHOOSE!

Would you rather...

HAVE 17 TESTICLES

JUST ONE TESTICLE
THE SIZE OF A CANTALOUPE?

Would you rather have sex with...

Gwyneth Paltrow **OR** Carmen Electra with a unibrow?

a toothless Kelly Clarkson **OR** a hairless Lucy Liu?

an albino Eva Longoria **OR** Katie Holmes slathered in mayo?

Lindsay Lohan 30 years from now **OR** Lindsay Lohan 10 years ago?

Elizabeth Hurley without the accent **OR** Beyoncé Knowles without the accent (i.e. Beyonce Knowles)?

YOU MUST CHOOSE!

Ménage a Troiseses

Would you rather have a three-way with...

Flavor Flav and Teri Hatcher **OR** Ted Koppel and Kelly Ripa?

Jennifer Connelly and Lawrence Taylor **OR** Blake Lively and Billy Bob Thornton's character in *Slingblade*?

the *Guinness Book of Records* World's Fattest Twins (the ones who are always shown on motorcycles) **OR** the *Guinness Book of Records* World's Tallest Man and World's Shortest Man?

Things to consider: Note to self: Idea for TV show: The fat twins on motorcycles become motorcycle cops; also: try to make sentence with as many colons as possible.

YOU MUST CHOOSE!

Would you rather...

get punched hard in the gut by the person on your left

OR

kissed passionately by the person on your right?

Would you rather have sex with...

a 5'2" version of Ashton Kutcher *OR* Jason Bateman if he put on 50 pounds?

a soft and tender Don Cheadle *OR* an excitingly rough Hamburglar?

Josh Duhamel without limbs *OR* Tobey Maguire with an extra one?

a chain smoking Kofi Annan *OR* Ben Kingsley playing kazoo?

YOU MUST CHOOSE!

Historical Friction

If you could go back in time, would you rather...

dance with Fred Astaire **OR** be serenaded by Frank Sinatra?

have Leonardo da Vinci paint your portrait **OR** have Shakespeare write you a sonnet?

have Mozart compose a symphony for you **OR** have Jeff Foxworthy compose a "You Might Be A Redneck If..." joke in your honor?

Would you rather...

get drunk-dialed by Gandhi

OR

by Martin Luther King, Jr.?

YOU MUST CHOOSE!

Would you rather...

have sex with Paris Hilton

OR

slap her in the face?

Would you rather...

play Electronic Battleship with Tyra Banks

OR

help Michelle Kwan assemble a bookshelf?

YOU MUST CHOOSE!

Putting the "Or" in "Orgy"

Would you rather attend an orgy with...

The McLaughlin Group **OR** the *60 Minutes* reporters?

whiny ninjas **OR** jolly sumo wrestlers?

bipolar pirates **OR** insecure jugglers?

obese clowns **OR** The Fry Guys?

The Keebler Elves **OR** the Rice Krispies Onomatopoeias?

YOU MUST CHOOSE!

Date, Marry, Or Screw

Here's an oldie but a goodie. We give you three names. You decide which one you'd marry, which you'd date, and which you'd screw.

Bill Clinton, George W. Bush, George H.W. Bush

Alec Baldwin, Stephen Baldwin, Daniel Baldwin

Michael Jackson circa *Thriller*, Michael Jackson circa *Bad*, Michael Jackson circa *This Is It*

Britney Spears, Jessica Simpson, Mariah Carey

Condoleezza Rice, Connie Chung, the hot Hooters waitress with low self esteem

YOU MUST CHOOSE!

Date, Marry, Screw, Play Ping Pong Against, or Create a Revolutionary Movement With?

Okay, you mastered that one. Now to challenge you, we've added a few more options and names, resulting in more permutations. Here you must decide, which name you'd marry, which you'd date, which you'd screw, which you'd play ping-pong against, and which you would start a revolutionary movement with.

Ben Affleck, Matt Damon, Che Guevara, ping pong champion John Hu, Mel Gibson

Tommy Lee, Ben Franklin, Tim Duncan, The Rock, Alan Greenspan

Courtney Cox, Lisa Kudrow, Jennifer Aniston, Deborah Messing, your mother

Al Sharpton, Corey Feldman, Corey Haim, Venus Williams, the girl at Starbucks who looks a little like Larry Bird

YOU MUST CHOOSE!

Pretty good, but can you handle this one?

Date, Marry, Screw, Discuss War of 1812 with, Accompany to Six Flags Amusement Park, or Collaborate to Write Hip Hop Album?

Jerome Bettis, Molly Ringwald, George Stephanoplous, Eminem, Menudo, God

UN Ambassador John Bolton, 50 Cent, Tiger Woods, The Teletubbies, Charlie Sheen, Roberto Benigni

Maria Shriver, Bill Wennington, Darth Maul, Hitler, a can of tennis balls, Gomberg

YOU MUST CHOOSE!

Would you rather...

have an 8-inch-wide innie belly-button

OR

have a 10-inch-long outie belly button?

Would you rather...

be caught masturbating by _____
(insert friend of the family)

OR

catch _____ masturbating?
(insert friend of the family)

YOU MUST CHOOSE!

Would you rather...

give analingus to _____
(insert unappealing acquaintance)

OR

lose your _____ ?
(insert body part)

YOU MUST CHOOSE!

Would you rather...

HAVE A PENIS THAT DOUBLES
AS A MICROPHONE

OR

HAVE A WORKING CABLE TV
VIDEO SCREEN ON YOUR TAINT?

Would you rather use as sex toys...

a tetherball, a map of Uruguay, and a Zhu Zhu pet

OR

some measuring spoons, a thermos, and a Mark Eaton rookie card?

YOU MUST CHOOSE!

Pornification

Pornographers are quick to capitalize on the success of mainstream movies. All it takes to turn an actual movie into a pornographic film is a slight tweak of the title.
This process is called "Pornification."

For example, *Good Will Hunting*, when pornified, becomes *Good Will Humping*. Similarly, *The Terminator* becomes, of course, *The Sperminator*.

For every legit movie, there exists (at least theoretically) a porn version of that movie.

Test your understanding of Pornification on the next two pages with our Pornification Quiz.

Here are some pornified titles. Can you figure out the original Hollywood film that inspired them?

Answers on page 296

1. *American Booty*

2. *Titty Lickers*

3. *Grinding Nemo*

Now, the fun part. We give you the popular movie title. Can you pornify it?

Answers on page 296

4. *The Nutty Professor*

5. *S.W.A.T.*

6. *Toy Story*

More titles to pornify.

Answers on page 296

7. *Big Trouble in Little China*

8. *Analyze This*

9. *Glory*

10. *Space Jam*

11. *Malcolm X*

12. *Chitty Chitty Bang Bang*

13. *Shaft*

14. *Cold Mountain*

15. *Lou Dobbs Moneyline*

Would you rather...

have an anus that can function as a DustBuster

OR

nipples that can act as universal light dimmers?

Would you rather...

have puma-like reactions with the remote control when watching something dirty, and someone walks into the room, and you need to change it

OR

have expert precision with the cheek-kiss greeting?

YOU MUST CHOOSE!

Would you rather...

have a stable of remarkably sympathetic woodland creatures to confide in about romantic desires and dreams

OR

be capable of ending any relationship tension-free with no ensuing debate or discussion by pulling out a red card like in soccer?

Things to consider: yellow card warnings

Would you rather...

during sex, be able to read the mind of the person you are having sex with

OR

be able to hit your or your partner's g-spot by finding Waldo in a *Where's Waldo* book? (each page can be used once)

YOU MUST CHOOSE!

Would you rather...

chew a used condom as gum for an hour

OR

wring out ten maxipads straight into your mouth?

Would you rather...

do a shot of bull semen

OR

taste a spoonful of horse afterbirth?

Would you rather...

have all your pubic hairs become ingrown

OR

receive a fire hose enema?

YOU MUST CHOOSE!

After a night of drunkenness, would you rather wake up next to...

a close co-worker **OR** a friend of your mother's?

your best friend of the opposite sex **OR** your very attractive first cousin?

the ugliest person from your high school **OR** that freaky mascot dude in the Burger King commercial?

YOU MUST CHOOSE!

These are the circumstances. You are stuck on a desert island. You pray to the Deity, and he allows you one possession.

Would you rather be stuck on a desert island with...

the complete works of Jane Austen **OR** a year's worth of *Barely Legal*?

your significant other and an iPod filled with Barry White's most sultry tunes **OR** your significant other and a complete set of *Magic: The Gathering* cards?

a fishing rod **OR** a funhouse mirror, a wig, and some KY jelly?

YOU MUST CHOOSE!

BE STUCK ON A DESERT ISLAND WITH SOCRATES

OR

JENNA JAMESON?

Would you rather...

be sexually abused by the monsters in *Where the Wild Things Are*

OR

get bukkaked by the Smurfs?

Things to consider: Papa, Hefty, Clumsy, Brainy Smurf's
a heavy cummer

Would you rather...

have your nipples gnawed off by a swarm of fire ants

OR

sit on an umbrella and then open it?

YOU MUST CHOOSE!

Would you rather...

have your genitals drawn and quartered

OR

have your urinary tract filled with cement?

Would you rather...

receive an enema with leech-infested water

OR

dry-hump a cheese grater naked?

YOU MUST CHOOSE!

Would you rather...

stick your schlong in the spokes of a spinning bike wheel **OR** a toaster slot?

a George Foreman Grill turned all the way up **OR** a car door right before slamming it?

a tank full of hungry piranhas **OR** a paper shredder?

in a bowl of liquid nitrogen lubricant **OR** on a tee for a Tiger Woods drive?

Would you rather...

perform oral sex on a chronic flatulator

OR

be manually stimulated by the man with the world's longest fingernails?

YOU MUST CHOOSE!

Would you rather...

give a blumpkin to Louie Anderson

OR

give Forest Whitaker a handjob?

You are searching through your parents' closet.

Would you rather find...

a home sex video of your parents *OR* a list of swinger clubs with grades written next to each listing?

Nina Hartley's *Guide to Anal Sex* *OR* your adoption papers?

edible undies *OR* copies of love letters from your mom to Baron Von Raschke?

YOU MUST CHOOSE!

186

Would you rather...

be double-teamed by mimes

OR

be wagon-trained by a quartet of sex-starved Ewoks?

Would you rather...

find a used condom at the bottom of your vanilla latté

OR

find a dirty panty liner under the cheese in your tuna melt?

YOU MUST CHOOSE!

Would you rather...

be donkey-punched by John Madden

OR

receive Arabian Goggles from the *WWE*'s Mark Henry?

Things to consider: what we have done with our elite college education

Would you rather be caught masturbating by...

your grandparents *OR* your parents?

a one-year-old *OR* your dog?

H.R. Pufnstuf *OR* the ghost of Frederick Douglass?

YOU MUST CHOOSE!

Would you rather...

as a guy, be licking a woman's breast only to discover a 3-inch hair on her nipple

OR

be kissing her lower back only to discover a tattoo of Ron Jaworski ?

Would you rather...

make out with someone in a dark club only to find when the lights go on that their mouth is covered in open puss-filled cold sores

OR

that it's your mother-in-law? Father-in-law? Kurt Rambis?

YOU MUST CHOOSE!

Would you rather...

have your mom bring a blacklight into your room to reveal the various sexual fluids strewn about

OR

have to call tech support because you were surfing porn and more and more porn sites and pop-ups keep coming up on screen and so you have to talk through the problem with specifics and you're like "this website Assparade.com comes up and when I try to close it, an ad for Peter North's Volume pills comes up," and your mom comes in, and you try to close all the sites and ads real quick, like you're playing Missile Command on Atari, but every time you close a window, another porn ad pops open, and it's like trying to cut off the Hydra's heads, and your turn off the monitor but it's too late, and you realize that maybe it's time to move out of your parents' house?

YOU MUST CHOOSE!

During sex, would you rather hear...

"Uh-oh" **OR** "What is that?!"?

"Oops" **OR** "That's where that is"?

a yawn **OR** "Oy vey"?

Would you rather...

have a scrotum that fills with fresh-popped popcorn upon getting aroused (à la Jiffy Pop)

OR

make the sound of a foghorn upon orgasm?

YOU MUST CHOOSE!

Would you rather...

defile your child's Winnie the Pooh hand puppet

OR

commit lewd acts on Teddy Ruxpin?

Would you rather...

have a website broadcast all your showers

OR

your bowel movements?

YOU MUST CHOOSE!

FIGHT FOR YOUR LOVE...

Sure, you're a lover not a fighter, but the Deity wants to see that you'd fight for your loved one. He's kidnapped your significant other and says you must defeat his minions gladiator-style in a fight to the death in a closed 20' by 20' room. All enemies are hostile.

Would you rather fight to the death...

50 remote control planes *OR* 1,000 hamsters?

1,000 sloths *OR* 80 penguins?

possessed office supplies *OR* possessed deli meats?

YOU MUST CHOOSE!

This Or That?

Challenge yourself or your friends with the following quiz.

Answers are on page 297.

1. Supreme Court Justice or Venereal Disease?

   a. Scalia

   b. Gonorrhea

   c. Chlamydia

   d. Bader Ginsberg

2. Bible Chapter or Porn Magazine?

   a. Revelation

   b. Cheri

   c. Genesis

   d. Barely Legal

3. *Batman* Villain or Dildo?

    a. The Penguin

    b. The Emperor

    c. The Joker

    d. The Tickler

4. Catskills Comedian or VD Symptom?

    a. Clammy Hands

    b. Shecky Green

    c. Swollen Glands

    d. Soupy Sales

5. '80s Movie or Euphemism for Sex?

    a. *Romancing the Stone*

    b. *Bumping Uglies*

    c. *Gleaming the Cube*

    d. *Burying the Purple Headed Warrior*

Let's get right to the point.

Would you... fuck the Michelin Man for a 64-inch flat screen plasma TV?

Would you... let a stranger have sex with your spouse for $100,000 dollars? $500,000? $2,000,000? What if that man was former NBA great Ralph Sampson?

Would you... bludgeon thirty baby seals to death to have sex with Penelope Cruz? Vice-versa?

YOU MUST CHOOSE!

Would you rather...

date someone with a razor sharp wit

OR

a vibrating tongue?

Would you rather...

only be able to pick up guys/chicks via middle-school-style notes folded with hearts

OR

by window-side serenades of hits from the early '80s?

Things to consider: creative I-dotting, *Total Eclipse of the Hear*t, *All Out of Love*, *Turning Japanese*, *Rocket*

YOU MUST CHOOSE!

Would you... give a hickey to your grandmother for $5,000?

Would you... want to be able to perform oral sex on yourself?

Things to consider: never wanting to leave the house, which leads to lack of exercise, which leads to weight gain, which leads to no longer being able to continue said ability.

YOU MUST CHOOSE!

Would you rather...

date someone with a winterbush (very heavy unkempt pubic hair)

OR

an autumnbush (hair that changes color and falls out in fall)?

Would you rather...

marry someone whose desired personal space was 2 inches

OR

30 feet?

YOU MUST CHOOSE!

Would you rather have sex with...

Ernie

Pro Bert – Justin Heimberg

Bert is a take-charge kind of guy. Ernie is submissive and inept at everything he does. He mistook a washtub for a hat. What makes you think he knows his way around a woman? Ernie is a giggly best friend, a sidekick. Bert is a romantic leading man. Bert is the strong, silent type: tall, yellow, and handsome. Plus, he's hung like a horse.

OR Bert?

Pro Ernie – David Gomberg

When making this decision one has to consider who would be more attentive to the needs of a woman. Clearly, the answer to this is Ernie. Ernie is one to please. Witness the dynamic between him and the more uptight Bert. Bert is high-maintenance. Bert is jaundiced. Bert is the kind of guy who would roll over and go to sleep. Ernie would cuddle with you. Ernie would tenderly sing you to sleep in his arms: "Rubber Ducky... you're the one..."

Would you rather have your love life written by...

the writers of *Grey's Anatomy* **OR** porn czar Seymore Butts?

Woody Allen **OR** Nicholas Sparks?

Charles Bukowski **OR** the producers of *Rock of Love*?

Would you rather...

your marriage counselor be Dr. Drew

OR

Dr. Dre?

YOU MUST CHOOSE!

Would you rather marry...

an ugly rock star **OR** a hot garbage man?

a rich, shallow investment banker **OR** a poor, brilliant artist?

a self-righteous milkman **OR** a melancholy locksmith?

a bipolar tour guide **OR** an autistic Foot Locker salesperson?

YOU MUST CHOOSE!

Would you rather...

have your wedding conducted in the tone of a rap video

OR

in the tone of an elementary school play?

Would you rather...

date someone who only wants to have sex once a month

OR

date someone who made you solve a riddle before moving to each new step sexually?

Things to consider: what is the angle between the hands of a clock if the clock shows 3:15? If you answered, 7.5 degrees, you may now fondle my breasts.

YOU MUST CHOOSE!

Would you rather...

spend your honeymoon in a Home Depot **OR** a bowling alley?

in a slaughterhouse **OR** at your mom's house?

at a four day Civil War reenactment **OR** at a Vietnam War reenactment?

For your wedding, would you rather...

be registered at Quiznos **OR** at the Chuck E. Cheese prize counter?

an S&M shop **OR** a D&D shop?

Leo's House of Gauze **OR** All Things Tungsten?

YOU MUST CHOOSE!

Indecent Proposals

Would you rather be proposed to...

in the *New York Times* crossword puzzle **OR** with skywriting?

on live TV **OR** with your Alpha-Bits cereal?

on the JumboTron screen at a baseball game **OR** be divorced on the JumboTron screen at a baseball game?

YOU MUST CHOOSE!

Would you rather...

Authors' Debate ◄

Special Non-Sex Question!

Would you rather...

have all your eyeblinks last 10 seconds

Anti-yawn – Justin Heimberg

Two-hour yawns create a paradoxical torture. A Catch-22 of the worst sort. Follow the logic, here. You yawn when you are tired. You cannot fall asleep when you are yawning. Ergo, you will never get any sleep. Your two-hour yawns will keep you up in that weird suspended animation-like state that is the yawn. You will then become more and more tired each hour, each day, increasingly yawning, increasingly prohibiting sleep. Eventually you will go crazy and wander the streets known as the Yawner, a creature of myth that people both yearn and fear to see. Your mouth will open and close on its own accord, making chewing impossible, until your diet will be all smoothies and the bugs that inevitbably will fly into your open yawning mouth. Eventually, hungry, infected wth mouth sores, and deprived of sleep, you will yawn yourself to death.

OR have all your yawns last two hours?

Anti-blink – David Gomberg

We blink often. An average of 20 times per minute, according to the second thing that came up when I Googled it. That means there are only a few seconds between blinks. Do the math. This means your eyes will be closed at a 3:1 ratio. Do the math. 10 seconds closed, 3 seconds open. You are half-blind, not in one eye, and not with bad vision, but half the time. Driving is an impossibility. I mean, do the math. Reading would be too arduous to deal with. You'd always be the one screwing up family pictures. Have you done your math homework? People will always think you are deep in thought and meditation only to emerge with uninteresting shallow thoughts. You'd be a constant blinking disappointment. Do the math. Seriously. Please.

Would you rather date...

a woman who loves to give oral sex, but while doing it, hums the tune to the *Sanford and Son* theme song

OR

a woman who talks filthy but speaks in the voice of Yosemite Sam?

Would you rather date...

a woman with a great body but simple conversational skills

OR

a woman who speaks with wit and insight but keeps her hand perpetually soaking in a bowl of wet spinach?

YOU MUST CHOOSE!

Would you rather your only pick-up line be...

"To answer your question—Yes. Light weights, high reps."

OR

"I want to bang you in your bunghole so my sperms don't go up your fallopians."?

The Deity has released a line of new colognes.

Would you rather wear...

New Tennis Ball **OR** Wet German Shepherd?

Mulch **OR** Pungent Reefer ?

Eau de Gomberg **OR** Eau de Heimberg?

YOU MUST CHOOSE!

On a first date with someone you really like, would you rather...

be unable to talk about anything other than the mechanism that causes grass stains

OR

have to use the phrase "white power" 20 times?

YOU MUST CHOOSE!

Would you rather...

play strip poker with _____
(insert three relatives)

OR

rub oil on every inch of _____ ?
(insert vile acquaintance)

Would you rather...

call up _____ , state your name,
(insert set of friend's parents)
and have phone sex

OR

take a shower with _____ ?
(insert somebody else's parents)

YOU MUST CHOOSE!

Would you rather...

HAVE SEX WITH A "10"

OR

FIVE "2"S?

Would you rather...

have your wedding vows written by gangsta rappers

OR

by the author of one of those African spam money request emails?

Things to consider: "It is of the utmost Urgency with which I submit this plea for your sincerest Love and Trustworthiness?"

For your wedding, would you rather...

have a paintball war at the reception

OR

enter down the aisle to the tune of "We're Not Gonna Take It" by Twisted Sister?

YOU MUST CHOOSE!

Would you... take the surname of your spouse upon marriage if it were "Vulvatron?"

Would you... add a "De" to the beginning of your first name (men)/change the last syllable of your first name to "eesha" (women) to be able to orgasm three times as intensely?

Would you... as a man, get breast implants for $300,000? (They can be removed after a year.)

YOU MUST CHOOSE!

Would you rather...

engage in heavy petting with _____
(insert head of state)

OR

dry hump _____ ?
(insert political satirist)

Would you rather...

play _____ with _____
(insert board game)   (insert hot celebrity)

OR

_____ with a _____
(insert verb)   (insert adjective)

_____ ?
(insert former San Diego Charger wide receiver)

YOU MUST CHOOSE!

Here's another fun one to try at home.

Would you rather...

stuff every orifice with dozens of shoe horns and Mr. T dolls while screaming "Resistance is Futile"

OR

dress up like a ringmaster while bakers whip you with cinnamon sticks and pour battery acid on your nipples, all while you malign the current French administration?

Would you rather...

have to make your Number 2's in the shower

OR

in mail slots?

YOU MUST CHOOSE!

Would you rather...

be incredibly charming, but only when discussing your bowel movements

OR

have an infallible pick-up line, but only with Fuddruckers employees?

Would you rather...

be found attractive by all members of the opposite sex, but secrete copious amounts of steak sauce when aroused

OR

have genitals that permanently tasted like chocolate, but have all your offspring be exact clones of Walter Matthau?

YOU MUST CHOOSE!

GAME: Below the Belt

Whoever is reading must convey the words below using charades. But here's the catch. You can only use your body from the waist down.

Doggie

Thrust

Five

Baseball

Poop

Pray

Rocket

Ejaculate

YOU MUST CHOOSE!

Would you rather...

have your sex drive vary directly with the strength of your cell phone reception

OR

vary directly with the moon phases, peaking at full moon?

Would you rather...

be completely infertile except when inside churches

OR

except when in bowling alleys?

YOU MUST CHOOSE!

Would you rather...

AFTER A NIGHT OF SEX,
WOULD YOU RATHER...
WAKE UP NEXT TO
YOUR FRIEND'S WIFE

OR

CHUCK E CHEESE?

Would you rather have sex with...

Chelsea Clinton **OR** a jaundiced Sandra Bullock?

an albino Freddie Prinze, Jr. **OR** a severely sun-burned Matt LeBlanc?

a 400-pound person on top **OR** a 300-pound person on crack?

WWE's Chyna **OR** Mandy Moore if she was missing an arm? Both arms? And a leg? Just a torso and a head?

Would you rather...

have pornographic pop-up ads constantly appearing in your thoughts

OR

have your cell phone wired into your body with the ring function set on "orgasm"?

YOU MUST CHOOSE!

Would you rather...

have your mom have to put on your condoms like she was dressing you as a child for the winter

OR

never be able to call your spouse by the same name twice?

Things to consider: coming up with new terms of endearment – Honey, Baby, Schnookeylups, Porko, Flartran, Sweetballs, Fatooshk

YOU MUST CHOOSE!

Would you... make out with and grope feverishly your best friend's mom for forty minutes for $45,000?

Would you... want a second portable set of "Voodoo doll" genitalia that communicates all sensation to your real genitalia?
Things to consider: theft, pets, surreptitious self-pleasure

YOU MUST CHOOSE!

Would you rather...

lactate Milwaukee's Best

OR

dental floss?

Would you rather...

have sex in front of your in-laws

OR

1,000 bloggers?

YOU MUST CHOOSE!

Would you rather live in a world where...

corporate hold music was phone sex

OR

Casual Friday was preceded by Thong Thursday?

Would you rather have sex with...

Maroon 5 *OR* Blink 182?

Sum 51 *OR* Matchbox 20?

Front 242 *OR* Florp 968?

YOU MUST CHOOSE!

Would you rather read...

Girls Gone Wild: The Novel

OR

Donkey Kong: The Novel

Girls Gone Wild: The Novel

She pried off the water-saturated mini-T-shirt, the last obstinate cling releasing like the inhibition she was shedding.

"Whoooo-hooooo-yeahhhh" bellowed the crowd who below her awaited their daily feeding of lascivious images like seals at Sea World.

"Whooo-hoo, yeahhhhh!" confirmed a posse of drunken members of the Kappa Sig fraternity who teetered on a balcony across the parade-laden street.

Spurred by the wanton courage of her compatriot, the young lady's peer delicately lifted her shirt, exposing part of one breast, and then quickly let the shirt recede to gravity's will.

"Seniors!" proffered a young man with vomit crusted on the corner of his mouth.

"Whoooo-Yeahhhhhhhh!" his friend added.

Donkey Kong: The Novel

He leaped with all his might over the rolling barrel, fighting to keep his eyes forward and not lift his gaze toward the captive damsel. The hammer hovering mere inches away, it was time to turn the tables. With a last vestige of energy, Mario grasped for the hammer and seized it with the determination of a plumber who had a problem to fix.

"Oh, if my brother Luigi could see me now," thought the mustachioed stereotype. BAM! The barrel was no match for the mighty swing of the stout and proud Italian. BAM! Another barrel was lost to the ether. Onward, Mario trod, the slight incline of the steel girder feeling like the slope of the mighty Everest.

And then he heard it. Whether it was the roar of a rolling barrel or the growl of the giant ape, Mario did not know.
What he had no doubts about whatsoever was that the sound shook him to his very core.

YOU MUST CHOOSE!

Would you rather your pimp be...

Mike Huckabee **OR** Emmanuel Lewis?

Grimace **OR** Chewbacca?

Vijay Singh **OR** Ben Bernanke?

YOU MUST CHOOSE!

Pick Your Scrotum!

Would you rather have...

a scrotum slightly too small for your testicles or a scrotum that was 40 times bigger than it is currently? (testicles remain the same size)

a transparent scrotum or a denim scrotum?

a plaid scrotum or a bungie-scrotum™?

Things to consider: other books that have an entire page dedicated to the scrotum: James Joyce's *Ulysses*, *Where's Waldo?*, the Bible, Jane Austen's *Scrotum*

YOU MUST CHOOSE!

Would you...

perform oral sex on _____

(insert undesirable acquaintance)

to have sex with _____ ?

(insert celebrity)

Would you rather...

tag on the phrase "for a girl" to every compliment you give
a female

OR

tag on a sarcastic "Sherlock" to every sexual exclamation
you utter?

YOU MUST CHOOSE!

Would you rather...

have testicles with the density of hydrogen

OR

of steel?

Would you rather...

think about sex every 6 or 7 seconds

OR

think about Chinese rice farmers tilling their fields every 6 or 7 seconds?

YOU MUST CHOOSE!

Would you rather...

turn into Sammy Davis, Jr. when masturbating

OR

have your sexual appetite vary directly with proximity to Radio Shack?

Would you rather...

have to use condoms that come in a wrapper where you have to finish the crossword puzzle before it can be opened

OR

be unable to shake the image of Meadowlark Lemon during all sexual congress?

YOU MUST CHOOSE!

Would you rather...

have the job of your dreams

Job of your dreams – David Gomberg

Imagine going to work and being excited about it. No more grind, no more slaving away with no validation or appreciation. Getting paid for what you love to do. It will improve your mood and the rest of your life as well. You spend more than half your waking life at work, and it's vital you enjoy what you do. Few of us get that chance. You'll be happy, as will your family and friends. You will excel in all areas of your life.

OR sit briefly on an omelet?

Sit on an omelet – Justin Heimberg

How do you know sitting on an omelet isn't the greatest thing in the world? Have you ever tried it? Didn't think so. Guess what? Sitting on an omelet *is* the best thing in the world. Way better than having the job of your dreams. Until you do it, you just won't get it. So go ahead, take that dream job. Knock yourself out. I'll be at home sitting on an omelet.

Would you rather have breast implants made of...

attracting magnets **OR** repelling magnets?

locusts **OR** throbbing hearts?

Brie cheese **OR** the spirit of Malcolm X?

YOU MUST CHOOSE!

Would you rather...

HAVE SEX WITH A WOMAN
WHO IS 2 FEET TALL

OR

10 FEET TALL?

Would you rather have sex with...

the Tin Man **OR** the Scarecrow?

Mr. Belvedere **OR** Matlock?

your dentist **OR** your 3rd grade PE teacher?

the "Where's the Beef" lady **OR** the "I've fallen and I can't get up!" lady?

Skeletor **OR** Gargamel?

YOU MUST CHOOSE!

Breastify!

Would you rather...

have 1 breast **OR** 3 breasts?

inverted concave breasts **OR** wildly cockeyed breasts?

snow globes for breasts **OR** magic eight balls?

the living heads of Cheech and Chong **OR** crystal balls where you can see the future (but only of the carpet industry)?

YOU MUST CHOOSE!

Would you rather...

utter all exclamations during sex in Shakespeare speak

OR

Haiku?

Things to Consider:

> oh yeah do me yeah
> like willow reed in cool pond
> pinch my nipple

Would you rather be unable to distinguish between...

hands and ears **OR** nipples and the TV remote control?

the phrases "I love you" and "goodbye" **OR** your significant other and Jim Lehrer?

your bedroom and Jamba Juice **OR** the texture smooth and the concept of ambivalence?

YOU MUST CHOOSE!

When you sleep, would you rather...

instead of REM (rapid eye movement), experience WTL (wild tongue lapping) **OR** have your penis move like a windshield wiper?

be a sleepwalker **OR** a sleephumper?

experience nocturnal tumescence **OR** nocturnal luminescence?

Would you rather...

receive a Cleveland Steamer from Brian Williams

OR

a Dirty Sanchez from former Postmaster General Marvin Runyon?

YOU MUST CHOOSE!

Would you rather...

have a horizontal buttcrack

OR

vertically aligned breasts?

(Dr. Seuss fans only)

Would you rather have sex with...

Salma Hayek on a kayak

OR

Halle Berry on a ferry? Penelope Cruz in grey ooze?

YOU MUST CHOOSE!

The Deity is going to give you an outfit to spice things up in the bedroom.

Would you rather...

wear bologna lingerie

OR

aviator glasses, crotchless acid wash jeans, and toy Hulk hands?

Would you rather...

be able to make your pubic hair grow in the pasta variety of your choice

OR

have the power to induce carnal fantasies about Nicolaus Copernicus?

Things to consider: rotini, penne, manicotti, gailileo

YOU MUST CHOOSE!

Pick Your Vagina!

Would you rather have a vagina...

that acts as a guillotine 1 out of every 8 times an object is inserted **OR** one that secretes sulfuric acid upon orgasm?

that doubles as a trash compactor **OR** a cassette player?

that howls like a wolf when the moon is full **OR** one that belts out the lyrics to Sinatra tunes on command?

YOU MUST CHOOSE!

Would you rather...

have tremendous sexual endurance but have no sense of feeling below your waist between the hours of 10 and 11 p.m.

OR

be an empathetic lover but be unwaveringly convinced that your significant other is a direct descendent of Leif Ericson?

Would you rather...

have two hours of private conversation with President Obama

OR

two minutes of private passion with Shakira?

YOU MUST CHOOSE!

Would you rather...

only be able to have sex with the aid of a golf caddie who gives you advice on your "strokes"

OR

only be able to have sex with the aid of a stern Romanian gymnastics coach screaming "YOU CAN DO IT!" from the sidelines?

YOU MUST CHOOSE!

The Deity encourages adventure in the bedroom between two consenting adults. You and your significant other are to participate in a role-playing fantasy...

Would you rather fantasize the scenario of...

"Rugged Cowboy Discovers Handmaiden in the Barn" **OR** "Cheerleader Approaches Bookish Professor After Class"?

"Secretary and Boss Working Late" **OR** "Tax Session with Accountant Ignites Passions"?

"Fan Meets Post-Concert Fabio" **OR** "Cashier Bumps Into Anonymous Thin Moroccan In Arby's Bathroom Stall"?

YOU MUST CHOOSE!

Would you rather...

ejaculate hot coffee

OR

crazy glue?

Would you rather...

spend two romantically charged hours with Martina Navratilova

OR

get a lap dance by a Sleestack from *Land of the Lost*?

YOU MUST CHOOSE!

Would you rather...

have phone sex with the teacher from the old *Charlie Brown* specials

OR

have telegraph sex? (see below for example)

PHONE SEX OPERATOR : I'm so horny STOP

YOU: What are you wearing STOP

PHONE SEX OPERATOR: Nothing STOP I'm so horny STOP

YOU: Oh yeah? STOP... (silence) No, I mean, don't stop. STOP... (silence)... Shit...

YOU MUST CHOOSE!

Would you rather have...

15 fingers **OR** 3 tongues?

57 testicles **OR** 1 testicle the size of a honeydew?

no nipples **OR** 11 nipples?

Things to consider: Reread now as "Would you rather date someone who had..."

Would you rather...

attract swarms of fireflies when aroused

OR

have the sound of microphone feedback intermittently emanating from your crotch?

YOU MUST CHOOSE!

Pick Your Pubes!

You can pick your friends, and you can pick your pubes, but you can't... wait, how does that go? Anyway...

Would you rather...

wear your pubic hair in a Fu-Manchu style **OR** ZZ Top beard style?

have pubes that lit up like fiber optic wires **OR** pubic hair that changes color to match your shirt?

pubes comprised of Brillo **OR** pubes that grow up and around your body like ivy on a house?

YOU MUST CHOOSE!

Would you rather have sex with...

just the top half of Briana Banks **OR** just the bottom half of Britney Spears?

the star of *Precious* **OR** Kate Beckinsale, 10 seconds after she passed away?

Topher Grace **OR** Kevin James? If they exchanged weights?

Would you rather...

have gratuitous Ted Danson cameos during erotic dreams

OR

have product placement in all your sexual fantasies?

YOU MUST CHOOSE!

Would you rather...

DATE A
HALF WOMAN/HALF HORSE

OR

HALF WOMAN/HALF COUCH?

Would you rather...

have sex with a woman with Kathy Bates's body on the top half and Carmen Electra's body on the bottom half

OR

Carmen Electra's body on top and Kathy Bates's on the bottom?

Would you rather always have to wear...

a spiked collar and black leather cap **OR** cherry Twizzler nipple piercings?

no underwear **OR** Green Lantern Underoos?

a sombrero **OR** a 10 pound Prince Albert?

YOU MUST CHOOSE!

Upon climax, would you rather...

shout out the names of various U.S. presidents **OR** Zagat's restaurant reviews?

the chorus to "Hava Nagila" **OR** the chorus to "Whoomp! There It Is"?

Monster Manual descriptions **OR** Barry Larkin's career statistics?

YOU MUST CHOOSE!

Would you rather have sex with...

Harrison Ford **OR** Han Solo?

Sean Penn **OR** Jeff Spicoli?

Hugh Jackman **OR** Wolverine?

Jeff Bridges **OR** The Dude?

Angelina Jolie **OR** Lara Croft?

YOU MUST CHOOSE!

Would you rather...

only be sexually aroused by people experiencing engine trouble

OR

having severe allergic reactions?

Would you rather live in a world where...

penis size fluctuates with interest rates

OR

where voting booths and porno peepshow booths
were the same thing?

YOU MUST CHOOSE!

Would you rather have sex with...

Batman **OR** Superman?

The Flash **OR** Spider-Man?

Toucan Sam **OR** Cap'n Crunch?

Things to consider: Cap'n Crunch's penchant for buggery

Would you rather have sex with...

The Bionic Woman **OR** Wilma from *Buck Rogers*?

Wonder Woman **OR** a real-life anatomically correct Barbie?

Snow White **OR** Rapunzel?

Things to consider: likely Rapunzel winterbush

YOU MUST CHOOSE!

Would you rather...

play this book with Adam Carolla

OR

John Ashcroft?

Would you rather have your only means of foreplay be...

cheek-kissing **OR** joint-fondling?

firm handshakes **OR** the ferocious tonguing of eyeballs?

political debate **OR** *Three's Company*-like misunderstandings?

YOU MUST CHOOSE!

Would You Rather...? *Ultimate Sex Edition*

Would you rather...

speak in the voice of a possessed Linda Blair in *The Exorcist* during sex

OR

compulsively yell out Starbucks orders in the heat of passion (for example, "Oh, yeah, oh yeah... Double Decaf Iced Mocha Frap!")?

YOU MUST CHOOSE!

Would you rather...

HAVE A SCROTUM THAT PUFFS UP LIKE A CAR AIR BAG WHEN YOU GET SCARED

OR

A BEAT-BOXING ANUS?

Would you rather...

your penis (men)/breasts (women) increase in size
by ten percent each year

OR

decrease in size by two percent each year?

Would you rather...

vicariously experience all orgasms that occur
in your ZIP code

OR

during sex, have the Microsoft paper clip help icon
appear with sex tips?

YOU MUST CHOOSE!

Would you rather...

have a scoop of vanilla ice cream encrusted with pubic hair trimmings

OR

a steaming slice of apple pie warmed with the flatulence of 1,000 chili-eating beer drinkers?

Would you rather...

cough anally

OR

fart orally? Excrete oculalry?

Things to consider: getting bronchitis

YOU MUST CHOOSE!

Would you rather...

HAVE MAGIC 8-BALLS
FOR ELBOWS

OR

SHRIMP FOR NIPPLES?

Would you rather have sex with...

Leonardo Dicaprio **OR** Russell Crowe?

old James Bond (Sean Connery in his prime) **OR** new James Bond (Daniel Craig)?

a soft and tender Tony Danza **OR** a fast and furious Mr. Peanut?

George Clooney **OR** John Goodman if they exchanged weights?

YOU MUST CHOOSE!

Would you rather...

give a feverish lap dance to _____
(insert friend's mom)

OR

get a feverish lap dance from _____ ?
(insert another friend's mom)

Would you rather...

fight _____
(insert tough acquaintance)

OR

have sex with _____ ?
(insert gross acquaintance)

YOU MUST CHOOSE!

Would you... passionately kiss _____ (insert relative)

to have sex with _____ ? (insert someone hot)

Would you rather...

have _____ pose naked until you have (insert friend or relative)

painted a reasonably accurate portrait

OR

meticulously moisturize, massage, and talc _____ ? (insert unattractive person)

YOU MUST CHOOSE!

Would you rather...

be bisexually attracted to men and fish

OR

tri-sexually attracted to men, women, and boxes of Milk Duds?

Would you rather...

have to solve a moderate-level Sudoku before unwrapping a condom

OR

only be able to maintain an erection (men)/reach orgasm (women) by singing the *Family Ties* theme song over and over?

YOU MUST CHOOSE!

Would you rather...

have sex with Hugh Jackman and get the mumps

OR

have sex with John Madden and get a $200 gift certificate to JCPenney?

Would you rather...

have sex with Zoe Saldana and lose a finger

OR

have sex with Janet Reno and gain permanent immunity from speeding tickets?

YOU MUST CHOOSE!

Would you rather...

have to masturbate wearing a condom

OR

have to masturbate to sex symbols pre-1979?

Upon orgasm, would you rather...

ejaculate au jus **OR** a small coiled novelty snake akin to those found in April Fool's peanut brittle jars?

a mist of Lysol **OR** Easy Cheese?

Skittles **OR** Broom Hilda dialogue bubbles?

YOU MUST CHOOSE!

Would you rather attend an orgy with...

your high school teachers **OR** middle school teachers?

The Super Friends **OR** X-Men?

people you know **OR** people you don't know?

Things to consider: "I'd never want to be part of an orgy that would take me as a member."

YOU MUST CHOOSE!

Would you rather...

eliminate PDA's (as in "public displays of affection")

OR

eliminate PDA's (as in people using "personal digital assistants" when in public)?

Would you rather...

(women read as "have a partner who has...")

have a penis that can change circumference size

OR

that can change length?

YOU MUST CHOOSE!

Would you rather...

have a three-way with Patrick Dempsey now
and '80s Patrick Dempsey circa *Can't By Me Love*

OR

River Phoenix when he was 18, and River Phoenix
if he were alive today?

YOU MUST CHOOSE!

Would you rather have sex with...

Kate Moss **OR** Fergie?

Judi Dench **OR** Tyra Banks if she was on fire?

Chloe Sevigny if she were deep-fried **OR** Leighton Meester if she had severe irritable bowl syndrome?

YOU MUST CHOOSE!

Would you rather have sex with...

McDreamy **OR** McSteamy?

McDonald **OR** McCheese?

MC Hammer **OR** MC Escher?

YOU MUST CHOOSE!

Would You Rather...? *Ultimate Sex Edition*

Would you rather...

have Nicholas Sparks write you a love letter

OR

be serenaded by Biz Markie?

Would you rather use as sex toys...

a wooden duck, a trident, and some balsamic vinaigrette

OR

a piano tie, a bag of croutons, a Gumby doll, and a Ronald Reagan mask?

YOU MUST CHOOSE!

Would you rather...

have an internal voice-over and montage where that *Inside the NFL* guy recounts and summarizes your sex life at the end of each week

OR

receive a private newspaper with full coverage of your sex life including forecasts and Op-Eds?

Would you rather...

your G-spot be located in your esophagus

OR

on each of your finger tips? Your eyeball?

YOU MUST CHOOSE!

Would you rather...

have a lover who is 6'4" with 32A breasts

OR

4'5" with 42HHH breasts?

Would you rather have sex with...

Tom Brady

OR

Webster if they exchanged heights?

YOU MUST CHOOSE!

Would you rather your only porn be...

John Hughes films **OR** Pert-Plus commercials?

sex symbols of the '70s **OR** '50s and '60s?

video game vixens **OR** imprecise memories of Deborah Norville circa 1985?

YOU MUST CHOOSE!

Would you rather...

have pubic hair that wriggled like worms

OR

a pube-blot (a different inkblot like pattern each day)?

Would you rather...

have a Flock of Seagulls-style haircut for your pubic hair

OR

a Rollie Fingers mustache style?

Things to consider: Other works that have dedicated an entire page to pubic hair – *Hamlet*, *Rapunzel 2: The Revenge*, the Articles of Confederation, *Where's Waldo?*, *Band of Brothers*

YOU MUST CHOOSE!

Would you rather...

have a three-way with TomKat (Tom Cruise, Katie Holmes)
OR Brangelina (Brad Pitt and Angelina Jolie)?

the old Bennifer (Ben Affleck and J-Lo)
OR the new Bennifer (Ben Affleck and Jennifer Garner)?

BobCat (Bob Saget and Catherine Zeta Jones)
OR Phillary (Dr. Phil and Hilary Duff)?

YOU MUST CHOOSE!

Would you rather...

give oral sex to your wife or girlfriend while menstruating

OR

have conversations about her weight and other sensitive topics during PMS?

Would you rather...

have a cell phone that is also an mp3 player and a camera

OR

that is also a boomerang and a vibrator?

Things to consider: speaker-phone phone sex, Safari trips

YOU MUST CHOOSE!

Would you rather...

have Monopoly® hotel and house boogers

OR

defecate Rubik's Snakes?

Things to consider: sneezing, position of Rubik's Snake upon egress: the line, the dog, the ball, the swan, etc.

Would you rather...

sneeze out of your ass

OR

fart out of your nose?

Things to consider: allergy season, crotch rot, skid marks in handkerchiefs

YOU MUST CHOOSE!

Would you rather...

have sex with a woman with Dr. Ruth Westheimer's body on the top half and Heidi Klum's body on the bottom half

OR

Heidi Klum's on top and Grimace's body on the bottom?

Would you rather...

have breast implants made of Jell-o

OR

that stress ball material?

YOU MUST CHOOSE!

Would you rather...

always have to wear ultra-ultra-low-riding jeans (waist-line is barely above the genitals and well below the pubic line)

Go Low! – Justin Heimberg

The lower the waistline, the better as far as I'm concerned. I'm not afraid of showing a little tuft. In fact, let's go right ahead and market them as "Tuft Jeans." Write the brand name in yellow stitching and a scraggly font that looks like pubic hair and everything. Slogan: "Just Enough Tuft." And on the flip side, having a little crack exposed isn't a bad idea either. It's a place to rest your cigarette. On the contrary, denim up to, and around, the nipples is like being in a straightjacket or worse, a unitard. You'd look like a merman. And imagine the nipple burn.

OR ultra-high-riding jeans (waist line is above the nipples)?

No Low! – David Gomberg

First of all, you do not want to see Heimberg's tuft. It's like staring at Medusa; you turn to stone. So just imagine the parade of pubic shrubbery one would be sentenced to see if Tuft Jeans hit the mass market. High-cinched jeans may limit mobility but they also act as a girdle giving a slimming effect. It's really just overalls without the straps. Granted they're super-tight overalls with a belt across the nipples, but who hasn't taken a belt across the nipples at some point, right?... Anyone?

Appendix: Real Editing Notes used During the Writing of this Book

1 – change a "dirty dolphin" to "Maestro"

14 – please put "elf-shoe" in quotes before "nipples"

31 – change to dreadlocks or pubic dreadlocks?

40 – need "have" before "your nipples"

69 – change sex with pack of Ewoks to sex with a beehive?

95 – change "Eisenhower shall return" to "Crack my toes!"

92 – in "boiling balls" questions, "water" needs to come after "boiling"

115 – in 13 anuses q, please add – "defecating would resemble Whack-a-mole"

116 – please change frog in your throat to stick up your ass

127 – change Neil Patrick Harris to "a koala bear"

136 – change second option to "use a used tampon to brew a mug of tea", thank you

139 – change dreadlocked pubes to "horrible camel toe, no matter what you wear" (dreadlocked pubes is a repeat)

149 – change "Rubik snake penis" to "an electric eel penis" (too many Rubik's Snake penis questions)

159 – can we please change "orphan child" to "flower seller"

171 – please change "have oral sex" with to "give analingus to"

171 – please change menorah to Zhu Zhu pet

175 – please change genitalia to an anus

183 – bukkaked (sp)

256 – add "pubes" before "comprised"

293 – need closing parenthesis after nipples

Answer Key

Answers to **Pornification**

1. *American Beauty*
2. *City Slickers*
3. *Finding Nemo*
4. *The Slutty Professor*
5. *T.W.A.T*
6. *Sex Toy Story* or *Boy Story*
7. *Big Trouble in Little Vagina*
8. *Analize This*
9. *Glory Hole*
10. *Face Jam*
11. *Malcolm XXX*
12. *Titty Titty Gang Bang*
13. *Shaft*
14. *Cold Mountin'*
15. *Lou Dobb's Money Shot*

Answers to **This or That?**

1. **a**. Supreme Court Justice **b**. Venereal Disease
   c. Venereal Disease **d**. Supreme Court Justice

2. **a**. Bible Chapter **b**. Porn Magazine **c**. Both
   d. Porn Magazine

3. **a**. *Batman* Villain **b**. Dildo **c**. *Batman* Villain **d**. Dildo

4. **a**. VD Symptom **b**. Catskills Comedian **c**. VD Symptom
   d. Catskills Comedian

5. **a**. '80s Movie **b**. Euphemism for Sex **c**. '80s Movie
   d. Euphemism for Sex

Answers to **Mystery Quiz**

1. Malted milk balls
2. 200 mg
3. False
4. Ed Begley, Jr.
5. Ed Begley, Sr.
6. No, thank you.
7. See 1, 4.

YOU MUST CHOOSE!

About the Authors

Justin Heimberg is an author and screenwriter living in suburban Maryland.

David Gomberg is a large, bipedal, insectoid aberration with an ape-like build. He has the ability to confuse any creature that sees all four of his eyes at once. He is often found in the Underdark, where he is sometimes captured and enslaved by other races, such as illithids. Despite his bestial appearance, Gomberg possesses a significant intelligence and language of his own.

Contact the authors at authors@sevenfooter.com

Would You Rather...? The Dirty Version

Finally, the *Would You Rather...?* book audiences have been calling for! The perfect ice-breaker, *Would You Rather...? The Dirty Version* explores the sexual, the seedy, the sardonic, and the silly in the unique hilarious tone that has helped sell over 700,000 *Would You Rather...?* books. Filled with pop culture references and celebrity-skewering, *The Dirty Version* will have you giggling and gagging alike as you and your

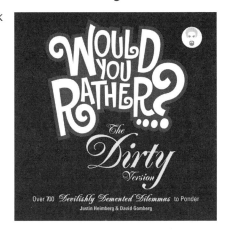

friends explore this no-holds-barred assortment of all-new devilish dilemmas, featuring questions like:

Would you rather... make out with your mom OR with a hot curling iron?

Would you rather... orgasm every time you sneeze OR sneeze every time you orgasm?

Would you rather... have cowgirl sex with a missionary OR missionary sex with a cowgirl?